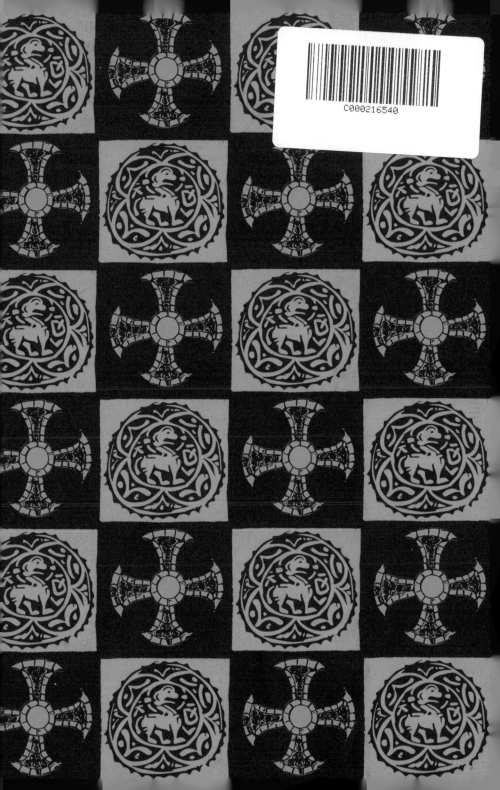

Charles Moseley

ETHELDREDA'S WORLD
PRINCESS, ABBESS, SAINT

CHARLES MOSELEY

MERLIN UNWIN BOOKS

First published in Great Britain by Merlin Unwin Books Ltd 2023

Merlin Unwin Books Ltd
Palmers House
Ludlow
Shropshire SY8 1DB
www.merlinunwin.co.uk

ISBN 978-1-913159-66-5
Typeset in 12 point ITC Galliard by Joanne Dovey, Merlin Unwin Books
Printed and bound by CPI Group (UK) Ltd, Croydon

Cover illustrations: Front: Medieval rood screen painting of St. Etheldreda, c.1500, St. Mary's, North Tuddenham, Norfolk
Back: The Trumpington Cross from the bed burial

Page illustrations designed from:
Page 3 Ironwork on the west door of Ely Cathedral
Page 4 Gold and niello belt buckle, Sutton Hoo c. 620
Page 7 Fives senses depicted on the Fuller Brooch
Page 21 Brooch from Chessel Down
Page 37 Aethelfrith of Mercia's ring
Page 64 The Trumpington Cross from the bed burial
Page 95 Pendant from the Harpole Cross
Page 102 Hunting Dogs from medieval stained glass in the porch of St. Mary's, North Tuddenham, Norfolk

Special thanks to the St Etheldreda Trust of Ely Place
at Holborn in London for sponsoring the
decorative endpapers of this book.

Contents

Wहат, wну
and whereføre

This short book is neither biography nor saint's life – they are not quite the same thing. It is an attempt to sketch something of the world in which that remarkable woman, who in 673 founded the first monastery at Ely, lived and operated. But in the end the past is unknowable. We find its traces in the writings it left behind, in buildings, in archaeology, but we cannot really know what it might have been like actually to *live* in those strange times, when almost nothing we take for granted was in place save birth, copulation and death. The world of our predecessors circled a different sun. One mildly amusing way of whiling away a wet afternoon is to list the daily things we think necessary that simply were not there even five hundred years ago, let alone 1300. What would life be like without potatoes or tomatoes, or tea or sugar, or pasta or paper, America, antibiotics or artificial fibres, coffee, mineral oil and plastics? As it happens, quite a lot of those we might list are not all that good for us. (Flush toilets are, if not terribly so for the environment.) We can make informed guesses around the bare facts, to be sure, but it was indeed a different country, and they did do things very differently. And made a go of it in ways which worked then.

Æþelþryð – let's use the Latin form of her name, Etheldreda, shall we, even if she never did? – and her relations left a huge mark on the land to which they had so recently come, and their consequences still reverberate in our present, just as ours will for our heirs in the unknowable future. By any standards she was a remarkable woman in a time of remarkable women, and far from being the wishy washy figure of so much (especially Victorian) stained glass she was – had to be – a tough operator.

Great saints are not pushovers. She knew, or was related to, almost everyone who was anyone in the Not-Yet-England of her time. She got her way. She changed the map. So it is worth thinking about what it was to be a Princess in that remarkable time when the England we know was beginning to be forged, an Abbess in a land where the old gods were still honoured by many when things got tough, (even if they were no longer openly worshipped), and what being revered as a Saint implies. For as T. S. Eliot makes his cynical Fourth Tempter say to Thomas à Becket in his play *Murder in the Cathedral*,

When King is dead, there's another King,
And one more King is another reign.
King is forgotten, when another shall come:
Saint and martyr rule from the tomb.

Her shadow is long. But we have to start a long way before
she begins to cast it.

Before we go further: there are lots of names, some rather like
each other, in this account, and a perhaps unfamiliar political
geography. So at the end, after having given due thanks to
all who have helped in making this book, I have added a sort
of survival kit: the people in the story and the important bit
of their interlocking networks, a timeline, and a summary of
what a map (if they had had maps, which they did not) of Not-
Yet-England would have looked like.

ETHELDREDA'S FOLK

A dozen or so generations before Etheldreda was born[1] (about 636) – the weather took a decided turn for the worse. It got colder: a lot colder. It got much wetter. And it kept on getting worse. In 536-40 and 547, a number of volcanic eruptions

---

[1] Probably in Exning near Newmarket. It is a day's walk from Ely, and was then almost on the boundary between the land of the East Saxons and that of the Southern Gyrwas. Her name means 'noble strength': fitting.
By the way, one of my guilty pleasures is footnotes. They are not intended to tell you what articles and books I have consulted, for this is not that sort of book. They are, really, just asides about things I thought interesting. Please be indulgent.

precipitated the worst volcanic winters in the last 2000 years and a drop in summer temperatures in Europe of up to 5ºC. Cultivation, which in the long preceding warmer period had spread to the more marginal lands and the higher latitudes of Europe to feed a growing and more affluent population, became more difficult. People started getting hungry, and hungry people are more prone to disease. And they get quarrelsome, and restless. Millions died.

That is part of the background to the extraordinary upheavals and mass migrations of people across Europe and Asia in the fifth and sixth centuries. These hungry people were being displaced by other hungry, and aggressive, people from further east. In the west the peoples of what we now call Frisia, Saxony, North Germany looked across the grey sea to the apparently kinder and richer land of Britannia. Many of their kin knew it well, of course, for they had been trading with it for generations, and some of the menfolk had taken service in the Roman army there. They began to come over with their families, then their extended families and thralls, to settle, first in small numbers, then in larger ones, and they were not always welcome even when there were tracts of land empty: Britannia too had suffered and many people had died of disease and starvation.[2] When I was at primary school we called this the Anglo Saxon invasions: but it was much less organised than that word implies. Think of them as boat people, refugees, a growing tide of them. In the fourth century the Romans built

---

[2] In AD 400 some calculate the population was some 3.6 million, of whom 125,000 were Roman army, their families and dependents. By 600 it was probably much less than half that, and even in 1000 it was only 1,250,000.

a chain of forts round the south-east coast, the Saxon Shore, to try to stop them. They failed. The migrants were our forebears.

By the late fifth century, when things started (and continued) going really wrong all over Europe, much of Gaul and Britain had been Christian for a good long while. Most of the newcomers were not. They worshipped the old Germanic gods, Thor the Thunderer (by far the most popular), one-eyed Woden the All-father, Freyja patroness of love, beauty, sex, but also of war, gold, magic and prophecy (her animal, it seems to me appropriately, is the cat), Tiw (war and combat, whose animal is a wolf) and Frey, associated with kingship, peace, weather and fertility. (Statuettes of Frey nearly always show him with a massive, indeed improbable, erection: forget about good manners in the ancient world.) To them sacrifice was made, of animals certainly, but also of men and women and children: we know that human sacrifice was still being offered in Uppsala in Sweden in the middle of the twelfth century, when a few hundred miles to the south, the miracle of Gothic stone was aspiring to express the Uncreated Light. Human sacrifice was far from unknown in the pagan parts of Not-Yet-England. Burials and cemeteries of the newcomers show that many of them were indeed pagan – though grave goods in some of the richer burials show that they had had contact with Christian realms like Byzantium.

These were Etheldreda's people – her ancestors just a few generations back. They were certainly not barbarians, with all that word implies, as most Roman and immediately post-Roman writers represent them. Their art, as the objects found in graves show, was among the best and most technically accomplished in Europe. They gave us the bones of the language we speak, they named our days of the week by the old gods. We call the greatest of Christian festivals by the name of their fertility goddess Eostre. They gave us a concept of law which grew into the Common Law, a bottom-up law, so to speak, rather than top-down like Roman. Their genes still live on in so many of us: if you work out that in Britain, into which there was no significant immigration between the Norman conquest of 1066 and the 1940s, everyone born (as I was) in that decade has at least 1,073,741,824 forebears. (There will be duplicates, of course.) It is easy to see that if we go back a further 500 years – when we have 35,184,372,088,832 – whenever we dig up a Saxon cemetery to build yet another housing estate the bones we find will be those of Auntie Æthel or Uncle Ecgbert.

They also brought with them their stories of lands on the cold Baltic shores they had left, their legends, their myths and epics, for it is by story and myth and ritual that a people creates and knows itself.[3] We do not know how many great poems there were – some may not have been written down – and only one has survived, its single MS rescued from a disastrous fire in Ashburnham House in London in 1731. We do not know that that survivor, *Beowulf*, was even the best, though its poetic techniques indicate a very sophisticated tradition indeed. But this great Old English poem is set in Sweden and

---

[3] Alcuin of York (who founded the Palace School at Charlemagne's capital, Aachen) writing c.797, complains about what monks read, especially the old stories and legends: 'Let the word of God be read in any gathering of priests, for there it is proper that the Word should be heard, not a lyre player, the words of the Fathers, not the songs of the gentiles. What has Ingeld [who appears in *Beowulf* and *Widsith*] to do with Christ?'

what is now Denmark, and never mentions Britain or the new land the Angles and Saxons have settled – rather as some of the best versions of ballads composed (God knows when) on the Scottish borders were found by researchers still being sung in the Appalachians of America a couple of centuries after the colonists had moved there and forgotten the rolling land between Solway and Tweed. *Beowulf* is relevant to our story, for, as we shall see, it is connected with Etheldreda: she may even have known – probably did know – a version of it.

The newcomers – all speaking versions of the same tongue, but from different homelands – settled, grew prosperous and powerful, and coalesced into little kingdoms, sometimes in alliance, sometimes at loggerheads. To the west were the Christian princedoms of the people who called themselves Cymry, 'The People', whom the newcomers called *wealhas,* which means 'foreigners': the Welsh. The West Saxons, the South Saxons, the East Saxons, the Middle Saxons, the East Angles, the People of the March (aka Mercia), the North Folk, the South Folk... we still remember those little family businesses (for family and lineage were crucial) in our county names.

Family: you were expected to know to whom you were related, even quite distantly. That simple fact radically alters how we can think about politics, society, relationships, culture. You could send a distinguished visitor with a letter of introduction – Roman Britain, and much of post-Roman Britain, was more literate than would be seen again for many a long year – to your cousin's cousin far away, confident that they would be hospitably received. And the Saxons, Jutes, and Angles also were used to, and needed, the same structures, and seem quickly to have formed more or less workable if not always amicable links with their immediate British neighbours. They fought from time to time. But of course they also talked to each other across the linguistic and cultural divide, even intermarried, and made alliances to bully a neighbour.

Family: when father says turn we all turn. These were hierarchical societies, with at the bottom the slaves or thralls, taken often on slaving raids. If the man who was prince or king at the time said you would become Christian, so you did. Moreover, we so easily forget the importance of networks: in a small society – say 1 million in all Not-Yet-England in about 600 – anybody who was anybody knew everyone else who was anybody. Which is why in 597 Pope Gregory the Great sent the mission of St Augustine to King Æðelberht of Kent, then the most powerful of all the Saxon kings, with a sort of overlordship up into what is now Yorkshire: a key man to convert, indeed, if you are thinking of top-down conversion. He was a pagan.

Too easily do people think *all* southern and eastern England was uniformly pagan until St Augustine came to Kent in 597. That is certainly not so. For example: the excavation in 2003 of the remarkable Prittlewell burial, now sacrificed to the demands of the Southend bypass, suggests that Christianity was already spreading among the Saxons: the dead man may have been Saexa, brother of Saebearht, King of the East Saxons. When they buried him about 580, they gave him the grave goods typical of a pagan burial, like the burial in Mound 1 at Sutton Hoo (610-635), but the gold crosses placed on his eyelids indicate he was Christian. And Augustine, an Italian monk of the new Order of St Benedict, was in for a pleasant surprise when he arrived. You may know the Venerable Bede's story in his wonderful *Ecclesiastical History of the English People* of how Pope Gregory the Great saw those blond Anglian children in the slave market: I was told it in the top class at primary school. Though Bede has him making other plays on words, apparently it's not quite true, and he did *not* say, neatly, 'non Angli sed angeli', which, according to John Hines, comes from a Victorian Latin prose school exercise[4]. For in a letter[5] of 595 Gregory asked his agent Candidus to buy Anglian slaves for training as monks so that they might become missionaries.

In the end it was the nervous, unwilling and fearful Augustine whom Gregory sent to Æthelbert. But his fears of this pagan prince turned out groundless: Æthelbert's queen, Bercta, a Merovingian princess, was already Christian, and worshipped in what was seen even then as an 'old' church in Canterbury, St Martin's. (There are indeed Roman bits in it.) Clearly there was already a considerable Christian element in the population of Britain, obeying its own bishops and having little to do with Rome but, it seems, quite a bit to do with Ireland. And Ireland is central in the conversion of the north, and important to what Etheldreda did in Ely.

---

[4] *'Anguli dicuntur illi de quibus sumus.' ille dixit, 'Angeli Dei'*
[5] VI. 10

One main written source of information for this period is Bede's great book, *Historia ecclesiastica gentis Anglorum* (*'Ecclesiastical History of the English People'*)[6] which he finished in 731. (He was born in about the year 673, when Etheldreda founded her monastery.) But he tells of the conversion of the great, the *powerful* people, the kings and princes: he hardly mentions the little people. Them we glimpse only *in the context* of the great, as when he praises the reign of Edwin, who first united Bernicia and Deira into Northumbria, as a time when a girl with a child on her hip and a bag of gold could safely walk alone across his realm.

We do, however, have to be somewhat careful of Bede, for his perspective is ethnocentric, devoutly catholic and politically Roman, and so he writes in elegant and persuasive prose a deceptively coherent and smooth account with all the wisdom of hindsight. First and foremost he is a *theological* writer of history, whose aim is to demonstrate the working out of God's purpose in human affairs, and that necessarily affects his selection and treatment of material. He implies the inevitability of the conversion of a people who are not yet self-identifying as 'English', and the necessary convergence with Rome. In fact nothing in history is inevitable before it has happened, and as always, things were much more untidy.

By no means all the newly settled Saxon and Anglian and Jutish kings and their councils were antagonistic to the missionaries – though the pagan priests with vested interests

---

[6] A small point, but when Bede writes *gentis Anglorum,* he is thinking of his own northern people, not 'English' in our sense, though later writers with a quite different agenda to his did try to construct it so.

might be. Some simply hedged their bets: like Rædwald, king of the East Angles (r. 599-624), probably the king who was buried in the great ship at Sutton Hoo, and after Augustine's Æthelbert died, the most powerful ruler – Bretwalda – in Not-Yet-England. Bede says that when Rædwald as a youth stayed with Æthelbert he became a Christian, but when he became king, fed up with nagging from his wife,

> ... *seduced by his wife and certain false teachers, and so being corrupted from the simplicity of the faith, his end was worse than his beginning. He seemed after the manner of the Samaritans of old to serve both Christ and the gods he served before. And so in one temple he had both an altar for the service of Christ and another little one for offering victims to devils. (II.15).[7]*

This anecdote not only hints at the influence a wife might have over her husband, but also shows that during the Conversion Christian and non-Christian worship might be practiced simultaneously. The 'little altar' (*arula*) survived into the time of Aldwulf, the king whom Bede knew.

Æthelbert, indeed, had welcomed Augustine's mission and converted – not, I am sure, simply to please his wife. In 620 their daughter Æthelburh was married to Edwin of Northumbria, still

---

[7] Bede never names his wife. And he presents her in a better light when she dissuades her husband – she must have been a woman with the gift of words – from dishonourably murdering the young, still pagan, Edwin of Northumbria, in flight from Æthelfrith (II.12). The history of this island would have been wholly different had she failed. There is speculation, which I find plausible, that Mound 14 at Sutton Hoo was hers.

a pagan, and now (with Rædwald's help) king. This was a politic move to protect his power in the north. One marriage condition was that she would be free to practise her own religion. (On her journey north, one of Augustine's Roman companions, Paulinus, first Bishop of Eoforwīc – our York – went with her. One would give a lot to know what they chatted about, that middle-aged man from Rome and the young Saxon princess. And, indeed, in what language.) Edwin was unquestionably a great and wise ruler. With the help of Rædwald, his ally and youthful mentor, he had greatly increased Northumbria's extent, swallowing up some of the smaller British princedoms. The huge timber palace at Yeavering near Wooler gives an idea of his glory.[8]

One of Bede's most famous stories is of Edwin calling a council in York in 627 to debate whether he and his kingdom should convert to his wife's faith. He made Paulinus – who became the first Bishop of York – address the meeting, and asked for comments. Coifi the priest said that the new faith was worth a try; after all, he said, no one had been more devoted to Woden and Thor and all the rest than he, and a fat lot of good it had done him. One of the chief thanes then spoke:

The life of man upon earth seems to me, in comparison with that time which is unknown to us, like to the flight of a sparrow through the hall wherein you sit at supper in winter, with your ealdormen and thegns, while the fire blazes in the midst warming us all, but the rain or snow are rages

---

[8] … the remains of which indicate many features that deliberately recall Roman structures – like an amphitheatre.

outside. The sparrow, flying in one door and immediately out at another, whilst inside, is safe from the tempest; but after a short space of fair weather, he vanishes out of your sight, passing from winter into winter again. So this life of man appears for a little while, but of what is to follow or what went before we know nothing at all. If, therefore, this new doctrine tells us something more certain, it seems justly to deserve to be followed.

Coifi spoke again: destroy the idols and their temples. Edwin agreed, and Coifi said, 'I will do this myself, for now that the true God has granted me knowledge, who more suitably than I can set a public example, and destroy the idols that I worshipped in ignorance?' He asked the king for arms and a stallion. 'Armed with both sword and spear, Coifi rode Edwin's horse to his own temple at Goodmanham, and cast a spear into it and profaned it.' (Bede, *H.E.* II:13).

Edwin's conversion was not the end of the story, of course: in 633, a mere six years afterwards, he died at Hatfield Chase in battle with the able and powerful pagan Penda of Mercia, and Penda in 642 also finished off his successor (St) Oswald. Indeed, Penda killed a good many kings: Rædwald's son, and also the enthusiastically Christian Anna of the East Angles, nephew of Rædwald. Anna was the father of several saintly daughters: Seaxburh, Æthelburh – and Etheldreda of Ely.

That tumultuous century from 580 to 680 – which covers all of Etheldreda's lifetime – was tough going: few died in their beds of the 16 kings in the two northern kingdoms of Bernicia and Deira. In 654 Oswiu, brother of Oswald, finally united them in the huge realm of Northumbria: and killed Penda at the climactic battle of the Winwæd in 655, somewhere near Leeds, perhaps near where the unheeding A1 on its way to join the M62 crosses the river Went. Bede says that that battle ended any organised pagan challenge to Christianity in the north.

The Christianisation of the pagan Saxon and Anglian kings actually happened very fast. The custom in Germanic societies of fostering your sons with another powerful family was a part of diplomacy, a way of building alliances and obligations, and the more powerful the house to which you sent your son the better. So was the trading of your daughters in marriage, often at a very early age, to cement an alliance. But it is also a very effective way of spreading ideas.

The conversion of the East and North of England is as much about family ties as it is of conviction. Even so, that has a flip side, and it was not all plain sailing from then on. For example, both Kent and Essex reverted to paganism on the deaths of Æthelbert of Kent and Saeberht of Essex in 616AD. Their sons, Eadbald in Kent and Saeberht's two sons, Sexred and Saeweard in Essex, immediately tried to repress Christianity, and banished the Bishop of London, Mellitus. (He had refused them the Eucharist after they had scoffed at its supposedly miraculous powers.)

All this momentous change is happening in the very years Etheldreda was growing up, and for those who were not making the decisions, life must have been very confusing indeed. Her father Anna was Rædwald's nephew, and heir after Rædwald's sons were killed in battle: this was the warlike line of the Wuffingas, whose palace at Rendlesham speaks of their power and the grave at Sutton Hoo of their wealth.[9] Their line traditionally stretched back beyond the migration period to a time in what is now Sweden and Denmark, and many scholars think that the poem *Beowulf* – or a version of what we have – was connected with their dynasty. And the Wuffingas traced their descent from Woden himself. (As indeed, does our own King Charles, through Cerdic the first prince of Wessex...)

Anna himself was not only a force to be reckoned with, but also a devout man who embraced the new faith enthusiastically, as did his daughters, all of whom came to be revered later as saints. But the life of a Saxon king was one of unremitting toil: intermittent warfare and rumour of warfare, keeping a wary eye on the neighbours, making sure you could keep your thegns happy with gifts (which meant the occasional raid would not come amiss). And so on.

Anna's East Anglia – I use the modern term, but they would have thought of it him as king of a people rather than a territory – was quite a plum in term of land and resources and access to the sea, and this is why an alliance with Eorcenberht of Kent, by the diplomatic marriage of his daughter Seaxburh, was useful for covering his back. Similar reasoning will have led him to marry a reluctant Etheldreda to Tondberct, the

---

[9] Among the objects recovered are Byzantine coins, Byzantine silverware, jade from the Far East, garnets from Sri Lanka.

prince of the Southern Gyrwas, who held Ely and the Fens on his western flank. For a nervous eye had to be kept northwest on Penda of Mercia: aggressive, ruthless, and something of a military genius. In 645, for example, Penda drove Cenwalh of Wessex from his kingdom – which promptly reverted to the old familiar gods: Cenwalh took refuge with Anna, where he converted to Christianity. (On his recovery of Wessex, Cenwalh re-established Christianity there.)

In 653, a year after Etheldreda's marriage, Penda attacked the East Angles with a large force and somewhere near Blythburgh defeated Anna, who with his son Jumin was killed in the slaughter. Anna's brother, Æthelhere, Etheldreda's uncle, took over as king. He did not last long, and died fighting on Penda's side at the climactic battle of the Winwæd in 655.

CHAPTER 2

PRINCESS

Etheldreda traditionally, and quite plausibly, was born at Exning, an important strategic centre just behind the huge barrier that we know as the Devil's Dyke. There is only one ancient crossing of the Dyke, where the Street Way (as one of the Icknield Way paths is known) pierces it, and it is within a mile of Exning.

Almost certainly it was Etheldreda's people who had the power and resources to build the Dyke. (The Devil only got into the story much later, for in the Middle Ages people called it simply le Micheldyche, 'The Great Dyke'.) It was constructed sometime between the 450s and the early 600s to block the Icknield Way, which for millennia had connected

Salisbury Plain with what is now Norfolk – and, who knows, perhaps once it went on down into lost Doggerland.[10]

Etheldreda's eldest sister, Seaxburh, was married off for political reasons to the King of Kent. After her husband died in 664, she ruled Kent until her son Ecgberht came of age. Then she became a nun, having as Queen regent founded the abbeys of Minster-in-Sheppey and Milton Regis. Another sister, Æthelburh, spent her life at the nunnery of Faremoutiers-en-Brie. Tradition has it there was a fourth daughter, Wihtburh, but Bede does not mention her and she first appears in a calendar in the late 10th century Bosworth Psalter. Seaxburh eventually succeeded Etheldreda as Abbess of Ely.

We can only guess at what being a child in a Saxon royal household might be like, and this is not a biography, so I won't speculate. What we can say as background is that even in a grand and important Saxon house there was very little privacy. People did not have separate rooms, or even beds. (Or deodorants.) The hall was where people got warm after being out in the cold, where they ate, sang, played games, slept when the trestle tables were moved away. In such a household, your rank was your wall for privacy: the high table for the most important, who had the precedence in taking food and drink, the fine robes and splendid jewels on which the changing firelight flashed and sparkled. For what it is worth,

---

[10] 7 miles from Fen edge at Reach to the headwaters of the Stour in what was thick forest at Woodditton. Date? Uncertain, but expecting trouble from the south west. Possibly sixth century, after the battle of Mount Badon – Lord know where that was, but it certainly happened – when the British thrashed the Saxons; or possibly later, to counter a threat from – guess where – Mercia. Three million man/days of shovelling chalk, it has been calculated... someone cared.

Etheldreda herself testifies later, obliquely, to her youthful delight in fine clothes and jewels – and necklaces: perhaps like the spectacularly rich Harpole necklace dating from this same period, found in the grave of a woman who was clearly important; or the necklace found in the grave in Ely of a 10- to 12-year-old girl of high rank. That dates from the very years when Etheldreda's monastery was getting going.

And so life at home would remain for many centuries. If you wanted to be confidential in your conversation, you went outside. The women would have their own quarters, but with equal lack of the privacy we would regard as basic. Much of their time, whatever their rank, they would be doing something with thread or cloth, for every piece of fabric, every stitch, had to be done by hand. And while it is pretty certain that, in addition to that, a peasant woman would also tend the fire and cook the food, it's interesting that while both women and men could be bakers, the word *coc*, 'cook', only occurs in a masculine form: it seems that professional cooking was mainly man's work. Food matters after all: our word 'Lord' descends from *hlaford* or *hlafweard*, 'keeper of the loaf', and 'Lady' from *hlafdige*, 'loaf kneader.'

We do know that like their father the girls were profoundly pious, and were powerfully attracted to life as nuns – as indeed they all became. It has been suggested that one person who influenced the girls was St Felix of Dunwich (*ob.* 647), a Burgundian who did much to evangelise the region and, as a powerful man in his own right, he must have had dealings with their father. Certainly they must have known of him. His relics were interred at Soham, between Ely and Exning, and remained there until the Vikings sacked the abbey he established: they were then carried off to Ramsey.

Later, we shall have to explore that word 'nun' a little. Like 'monastery', it does not mean what we mean when we use it after so many centuries of developing practice and familiarity. What needs some discussion before we go further is the place women had generally in Saxon society. There were women who were thralls, and with few rights – the concept of 'rights' hardly existed anyway – some of whom were exploited and abused: but free women were near equal companions to the males in their lives, husbands and brothers, much more so than in any other era before modern times. The wergild – the money payment if you killed someone – of a woman was usually equal to, and often more than, that of a man of the same class; in some areas, a free woman's wergild might be double a man's. (Slaves had no wergild, but had value: in Ælfred the Great's time, they were worth £1, the cost of eight oxen.)[11]

Women were expected to take responsibility, and palpably did so, as the historical record bears out. Women of status certainly had an honoured place in society, and could act on their own initiative. In *Beowulf*, as all the warriors are feasting in Heorot, the great mead hall, Wealtheow, Hrothgar's the king's wife, is honoured, tactful, a peacemaker after an ugly

---

[11] Like all ancient societies, that of Britain relied on slaves. The fortunes of war, raiding... there are several examples from Etheldreda's time of nobles and princes being taken in war and enslaved. It could sometimes go the other way: Bealhildis, or Bathild, just a half dozen years older than Etheldreda, and of the East Anglian royal house, was sold into slavery, was noticed by Clovis II and became his Queen in Neustria, and, as Queen, her piety led her to endow abbeys such as Jumièges and Luxeuil.

incident. The great Ælfred's daughter, Æthelflaed, known as the Lady of the Mercians, ruled that kingdom after her husband was killed, and was the brains behind the successful checking of the Danish offensive. Hild of Whitby, Etheldreda's aunt by marriage[12], was a key player at the crucial Synod held in the Abbey she founded, which was to decide whether the church in Not-Yet-England would follow the path of Rome or of Ireland.

There were, of course, some women of power who were pretty deplorable: for example, Cwēnþryð (or Quendreda), daughter of Coenwulf of Mercia, murdered her seven-year-old brother Kenelm who had succeeded to the throne. This may simply have been good politics: after all, the Bible warns, 'Woe to the land whose king is a child!', and a minority is often the recipe for disaster. (She was also Abbess of Minster-in-Thanet, but only because Coenwulf had established it as part of the patrimony of his family.) Æbbe, granddaughter of Edwin, sister of (St) Oswald and Oswiu, had a youth partly on the run from those who had killed her father, king of Deira. In exile in Dalriata (which included Iona) at the court of its king Eochaid Buidhe, she and her brothers converted to Christianity. When Oswald won the crown and things were safer for her, she established a double monastery for monks and nuns near the windy promontory of St Abb's Head: excavations reported in 2019 suggest that though

---

[12] Hild was the great Edwin's great-niece. Her elder sister, Hereswith, married Ethelric, brother of Anna of the East Angles, and the girls had partly been brought up in the household of Rædwald of the East Angles. It was the Danes who called it Whitby (and sacked the abbey, of course). Its Saxon name was Streanæshalch, which Bede interprets as Lighthouse Bay. The meaning is actually uncertain.

it was burnt by the Danes in that terrible year of 870 and abandoned, the new Norman monastery of Coldingham is roughly on the same site. She strongly supported and extended the missionary work St Aidan had started from Lindisfarne after being summoned there from Iona by King Oswald. Her political and pastoral skills were very influential, indeed pivotal, in Etheldreda's later career.

So Etheldreda's reluctant marriage at 16 followed the usual expectations of a princely alliance. And those would have been expectations she shared, as consonant with her status. The fact that in its arrangement she would have had, like so many other women of status and rank, no agency, does not mean she *felt* oppressed: her *mentalité*, like that of so many like her, was not ours. It was 'what people like us do.'

As we have seen, that did not deny such women a good deal of clout in their new role. For example, she, like others, could have quite a say, even initiative, in the management of affairs, and she did manage to arrange with Tondberct, who was a good deal older, to respect the vow of perpetual virginity, to be a mystical bride only of Christ, that she had made long before their marriage (which indicates that he shared her faith). What mattered was the alliance of the two realms, and he may not have been too bothered by this promise – after all, concubines were not hard to come by. He died in 655, three years after the marriage, but (so the usual story goes[13]) not before giving her, as was customary in

---

[13] It has been questioned by A. Thacker in the *Oxford Dictionary of National Biography* and 'The making of a local saint', *Local saints and local churches in the early medieval west*, ed. A. Thacker and R. Sharpe (2002), 45–74.

many Germanic societies, a 'morning gift' after the wedding night: the land we know as the Isle of Ely, 600 hides[14], Bede says, of good rich land, surrounded by the wealth of the Fen in fish and fowl and fuel. It may well have been part of the settlement negotiated between Anna and Tondberct, and certainly marked a major a shift of political influence as well as territory to the East Angles.

Ely was a rich 'gift' indeed. It was already populated and cultivated. If you guesstimate an average peasant family of 4, Bede's 600 hides give you a possible population of roughly 2,400 people, which, if you put them all near the site of the modern city, would give it a population double what the Poll Tax returns record for Ely in 1381. Even if you spread that number over the whole Isle, you still have in the context of Not-Yet-England a very well-populated and rich place.[15] Somewhere south of the present city there was a village called Cratendune, on the precise site of which nobody can yet agree[16], and the still serviceable Roman road running north from what we call Cambridge to the coast crossed the island.

---

[14] A hide is enough land to support a free peasant family. For comparison, Hild was given 40 hides for her Abbey at Whitby. What Tondberct gave was pretty certainly the actual island, surrounded by fen and water, not the much larger later administrative area of the Isle of Ely.

[15] From Tondberct's marriage gift stems the status of the Isle as a Palatinate jurisdiction, whose Bishop was a prince whose peace it was you broke (if so inclined), rather than the King's. Other palatinates included Durham, Chester and Lancaster – important counties on the Marches against the Welsh and the Scots, here the prince ruled semi-autonomously. Only in the second third of the 19th century were these palatinate jurisdictions abolished.

[16] A field south of Ely in the early 19th century was called Cratendon: that may be a memory of the old village.

It is likely that Tondberct had there a *villa regalis,* or royal estate, and it is probable that it is that residence to which Etheldreda returned when she came back from the north.

In the south aisle of Ely cathedral are two fragments of a cross – actually, the oldest things in the place. It cannot have been an elaborate object – I have seen far more flamboyant fragments of crosses of the same period treasured in parish churches across the north country. But these fragments connect with a real person on whom the young princess and the older abbess relied heavily, and about whom we know quite a lot.

The stones came from the village where the Isle of Ely presents its steepest face to the encircling Fen. One was being used as a mounting block on a farm in Haddenham: why waste a good bit of stone even if it had been a cross? On it is an inscription, faint now: LUCEM TUAM OVINO DA DEUS REQUIEM AMEN – 'Lord God, grant thy light and peace to Ovin. Amen.' And after 13 centuries he still has a place in the story, though he wrote no books, conquered no lands, and made small noise in the world save in the quiet humility of faithful service.

Ovin was born in the Fens, about 620. By the time he was 21, Tondberct had recognised his administrative ability, to the extent that Ovin was managing for him a large chunk of the Fens. In 652 on her marriage he will first have met Etheldreda. When Tondberct died, Etheldreda, also having lost her father killed in battle, made Ovin her bailiff – Bede calls him 'the chief of her thanes' – and relied on him to manage her large estate and care for its people, so that she and some companions could devote themselves to prayer and meditation. Later, he becomes a key figure in what she did in Ely.

But circumstances change, and a peaceful devout life in Ely was not to be. When Penda of Mercia was killed at the battle of the Winwæd, the two great Christian kingdoms of Northumbria and East Anglia could draw closer together. Royal women were indeed as good as any treaty: so, in 660, Etheldreda, now 24, was 'persuaded' by her uncle Æthelwold, now king of the East Angles, to cement this alliance more firmly.[17]

She was sent north to marry the fifteen-year-old Ecgfrith, Oswiu's heir to Northumbria. This ill-matched union was bound to fail as a marriage if not as a political strategy. It was Ovin who managed her journey and attended the wedding, conducted by (St) Wilfrid in York. That was probably the first time these two forceful young people, Etheldreda and Wilfrid, met. That energetic and maddening man (if you did not agree with him) was just about her age. Wilfrid (633-710) had been born in a noble Northumbrian family, and never lost – never in public tried to lose – a certain high-handedness and ostentatiousness of manner.

---

[17] The East Anglian royal house already had strong dynastic links with that of Northumbria, through the marriage of another of Etheldreda's paternal uncles with the Deiran princess Hereswith. She was the mother of Aldwulf, who in 664 succeeded his uncle as king of the East Angles, and cousin to Oswiu's queen, Eanflæd, and sister of Hild of Whitby. (I know, I know, too many names...)

He trained as a monk at Lindisfarne in the Irish tradition, moved to Canterbury, then on to Francia, then travelled to Rome where he became convinced of the Roman position for which he so successfully argued at the great Synod of Whitby called by Ecgfrith's father Oswiu in 664.[18] Wilfrid's stormy life included twice being expelled from Northumbria by its kings and having his property confiscated. So he went and bothered what is now Hampshire instead. (Eventually he got his monasteries of Ripon and Hexham back.) He was to play a very large part indeed in Etheldreda's life, and in the honour paid to her after her death.

---

[18] Just to fill in the background: In 664 King Oswiu called the Synod, about which I remember Miss Murphy telling us when we were in the top class at Beach Road County Primary School, to settle a growing problem: the Celtic, or Irish, church – the parent of Lindisfarne and a hugely energetic missionary church – differed in many practices from the Roman church. (Hild, abbess and founder at Whitby, herself of the royal house, had been called by Aidan of Lindisfarne to the religious life.) At issue were, first, the date of Easter: the Celtic church, relying on St John's Gospel, held it on the fourteenth day of the Jewish New Year (the date of the Crucifixion) which did not always fall on a Sunday; Rome, after the decision at the Council of Nicaea (325), held that it must be on a Sunday, that Jewish tradition did not bind Christians, and that it should fall on the first Sunday after the first full moon after the Spring Equinox.

As Easter determines the whole liturgical year, this difference mattered: for example, Oswiu, baptised in the Celtic tradition, kept the Easter feast, while his queen Eanflaed, brought up in the Roman tradition, was still deep in the fast of Lent. But the issues were wider: at bottom was whether the authority of Rome would take precedence over the looser organisation and slightly different rites of the Irish. Wilfrid argued the case for the Roman, and Bishop Colman of Lindisfarne for the Celtic tradition. Famously, Oswin asked, 'Who is the gatekeeper of heaven?' Everyone could agree on St Peter, and the Popes claimed to be his successors. It was to Wilfrid the King deferred. It all sounds so academic and remote, fit only for a footnote. But on that decision the whole future development of Church and State in Britain took a new and decisive direction: to what we are NOW. That is not to say that something valuable was not lost, which many are now painstakingly trying to recover.

On the whole, travel by water along the rivers, when possible, was preferred as it was much more comfortable and often quicker than going by land. To get to York by water would have been possible from Ely: a boat down-river to the Wash, and then a seagoing vessel up to the Humber and then up the Ouse to York.

What route Etheldreda's party could have taken if they went by land is also fairly clear from the route she took when she returned to Ely. The Roman road (the present A15, more or less) to Lincoln from Peterborough continues to meet the Humber near Winteringham. Then a ferry to Brough and then another Roman road to York. But first, a boat would be needed from the Isle to where they could join the main route north: possibly near Ramsey. (Some Roman roads, like the Great North Road or A1, may follow an even older line, for rich Britannia was not without roads before they came.)

Land travel in the seventh century was not that difficult, for though they had had little maintenance, the Roman network of roads was so well surveyed and built that it was still usable. The time when the roads get really terrible is the later mediaeval period – after all, in 1066, King Harold was able to do a phenomenal forced march along the Great Road to the North from London to Stamford Bridge, which is 180 miles, in just four days to deal with the Norwegian invasion. All that had changed, perhaps, was that the Roman practice of clearing the encroaching woodland along the line for some 50 yards on each side – an important security measure – had not happened. It would not be that wise if you were a person of importance to travel without a retinue, and we can be sure that by land (or water) Etheldreda's was pretty large. By land the party might make some 20 to 25 miles a day, for it had to go at the pace of the slowest, and would carry a lot of baggage with it. Harbingers would be sent ahead to arrange supplies of food and drink, and fodder for the horses, and places to sleep. Carts, when used, were unsprung and must have been dreadfully uncomfortable. A person of real standing might be carried in a litter: more comfortable, but slow. However they went, Ovin's management of the logistics of the journey must have been quite a daunting task.

Wilfrid supported Etheldreda in her single-minded dedication to virginity, and together they extracted the same undertaking from her new husband Ecgfrith which Tondberct, her first, had accepted. Ecgfrith was still a very young lad, and, faced with a very forceful, imperious and much older woman – and 24 looks ancient to the eyes of 15 – backed by a very tough bishop, initially he agreed she could remain a virgin.

She spent much of her time in prayer and fasting. She delighted in the company of monks and nuns, and invited to her house those who were most distinguished by learning and piety. They included the young Prior of Lindisfarne, (St) Cuthbert, to which monastery she gave many gifts from her own private property. Desiring to give him an even greater token of her regard, and to be specially remembered in his prayers, she also made an embroidered stole and a maniple for him. He said he would wear them only in the presence of God, to be reminded of her while celebrating Mass. As queen, she also took the momentous step of giving Wilfrid the large estate which her husband given her – much as Tondberct had given her Ely. It was there Wilfrid founded his great new monastery of Hexham. At the time some said it was the fairest church north of the Alps. (His stone throne is still there, in the chancel. It is not especially comfortable.)

But when Oswin died in 670, Ecgfrith, now 24 and king, and his advisers, were increasingly worried about the pressing need for a legitimate heir to secure the succession. Etheldreda, unwilling to break her vow in order to provide one, took herself off to Æbbe's new monastery. The abrasive Wilfrid supported, even encouraged, her: as he himself told Bede, despite all Ecgfrith could say, he used his influence with the queen at that time to strengthen her resolve to maintain her vow of virginity. This did not increase his popularity, already low, with the king.

In about 672 Ecgfrith decided to try to consummate the marriage, by force if necessary. He even attempted to bribe – not a good idea! – Wilfrid to use his influence on his queen to persuade her to relax and think of Northumbria… This failed. Instead, Wilfrid consecrated her as a nun, giving her the veil himself. So the king tried to take his queen from the monastery by force, but the story says that she was saved by a miraculous rising of the tide so that the posse could not get to the monastery.[19] Etheldreda fled south, to Ely, crossing the Humber near Stow, with two faithful nuns. Æbbe in the

---

[19] A similar story was told of Aebbe herself when she was pursued by a young noble called Aidan. Etheldreda, now 36, might anyway have been rather old to provide a clutch of heirs, quite apart from the risk to her of childbearing.
If Etheldreda had taken refuge on the headland itself, the flood is just about plausible in a very great storm surge, but certainly not at Coldingham. But miracles are part and parcel of the generic Saint's Life.

end managed to broker an uneasy peace between Wilfrid and Ecgfrith, but they never managed to get on. The marriage was annulled on the grounds of non-consummation in 672, and the king was free to take another, less challenging, wife.[20]

Think of those two spiky but impressive women, Æbbe and Etheldreda, when next you walk over from Coldingham to St Abb's Head on the springtime turf scattered with seapinks to watch the yearly miracle of the seabirds. They heard that incessant noise, they smelt that pungent smell from the hosts of nests, they too heard the sea rhythmically swashing in and out of the geos.

'She fled south to Ely'… What a complex of difficult questions that easy sentence glosses over! She was unquestionably Lady of the Isle, but what did the Isle, so to speak, 'mean' to her, her contemporaries and predecessors? How was it perceived? There may be more to that return then meets the eye.

Where water adjoins land is often a curiously ambivalent, in-between place – and water, especially springs, are often seen as somehow holy. (I can understand why: I know one spring near here where the people go quite thoughtful, as the water trickles out of the foot of the chalk scarp and begins its life-giving journey to the sea.) There are hosts of examples of ritual deposition, from at least the Bronze Age, of valued objects in

---

[20] Eormenburg, ironically, gave him no children and he was succeeded by his half-brother.

well and water and bog from all over northern Europe: near Ely, think only of Flag Fen near Peterborough. Islands too have a special resonance, especially islands that are near to but visible from other land: I think of Rousay and its many tombs in Orkney, Iona, Lindisfarne, Heligoland, Sark, Man – even Delos in the Aegean. Quite often they seem to become sacred or, at least, truce places. Now Ely does do lots of bog and water rather well, and there have been several finds on the water/land boundary round it of ritual deposition well into the Roman period. It is very tempting to see Ely as anciently a holy island, as a sacred entity, and the 'monastery' as encompassing the whole island – as in Lindisfarne, or Iona, or Crowland (which was also given in its entirety to a saint, Guthlac).

Many of those places, already inhabited, already sacred, were taken over seamlessly into being a Christian holy place, as Iona was. Furthermore, if you wish to think where you might place important buildings or spaces within the sacred area, it is a good rule to look at where the springs are. And being in a 'sacred' space does not mean people there, whole communities, do not get on with everyday normal tasks, for they always need doing. A religious community would include all those lay people who depended on it and on whom it depended.

Returning south to her isle and deciding to devote her life to God looks very different if you see the place as already holy, to which men and women of like mind and passion with her will follow this charismatic woman's leading and build a community. Being a nun was, also, empowerment.

Ovin had remained in the north for a time, and came to the point where he seems to have determined to follow the religious life. He presented himself to (St) Chad, then Abbot at Lastingham, carrying a spade and mattock. This was to indicate that he was no scholar, but came to do humble manual work in that monastery. The two men got on: when Chad became Abbot of Lichfield, in the heart of what had been Penda's kingdom, Ovin went south with him. But Chad died in 672, just when Ovin got news that Etheldreda was coming back to Ely with a plan to establish a double monastery for monks and nuns.

Usually, in such foundations, the women would outnumber the men, who would act as chaplains, and do a lot of the harder physical work in field and farm. She had ample resources from Tondberct's gift to fund this, and to support a community.

Ovin immediately came over to help with all the practical business of building her community and managing her familiar fields. The first church might well have been a wooden structure, though Bede does mention really high status buildings like churches being built *more Romanorum,* 'in the Roman fashion', in stone. A lot would depend on whether stone was available, and it is notably scarce in Ely. Cannibalising a Roman building, if there was one to hand, was not infrequent.[21]

She supervised her community until her death at 43 in 679. Ovin was then in his late fifties, and it is thought he returned to his own estate, perhaps at Haddenham a few miles from Ely, where he died. What one would give to know of the relationship of those two remarkable people!

---

[21] But see page 57.

CHAPTER 3

ABBESS

Imagine: in a year just before 700 you have heard of Etheldreda's sanctity (how could you not!) and you are visiting her new foundation and shrine on the Isle of Ely. What would you have seen, felt, smelt, heard as you made your way to the holy Isle?

We have a very, very much later account of what the old fenland was like from Charles Kingsley, who wrote *Hereward the Wake* about that Saxon hero's resistance, based in the fastness of Ely, to the Norman conquest. (It is dated, but still it is a well-made yarn and well worth reading. I read it as a child and hugely enjoyed it, for my default position was already almost by nature on the side of lost causes.) Like most of his generation he recognised the benefits of railways and steam engines which had made draining the fens vastly more efficient, but regretted the old Fens and what had been lost by new wholesale draining. He evoked the approach from the North by rail in an eloquent lecture to a Mechanics' Institute in Cambridge in 1867. He had watched the destruction of a great natural phenomenon, which had turned 'a waste howling wilderness' (the Great Fen was seen as such in his boyhood), into a 'Garden of the Lord, where

> *All the land in flowery squares*
> *Beneath a broad and equalblowing wind*
> *Smells of the coming summer.*

And yet the fancy may linger without blame, over the shining meres, the golden reedbeds, the countless waterfowl, the strange and gaudy insects, the wild nature, the mystery, the majesty – for mystery and majesty there were – which haunted the deep fens for many hundred years. Little thinks the Scotsman, whirled down by the Great Northern Railway from Peterborough to Huntingdon, what a grand place, even twenty years ago, was that Holme and Whittlesea, which is now but a black unsightly steaming flat, from which the meres and reedbeds of the old world are gone, while the corn and roots of the new world have not as yet taken their place.

But grand enough it was, that black ugly place, when backed by Caistor Hanglands and Holme Wood and the patches of the primeval forest; while dark green alders, and pale green reeds, stretched for miles round the broad lagoon, where the coot clanked, and the bittern boomed, and the sedgebird, not content with its own sweet song, mocked the notes of all the birds around; while high overhead hung motionless, hawk beyond hawk, buzzard beyond buzzard, kite beyond kite, as far as eye could see. Far off, upon the silver mere, would rise a puff of smoke from a punt, invisible from its flatness and white paint. Then down the wind came the boom of the great stanchion gun; and after that sound, another sound, louder as it neared; a cry as of all the bells of Cambridge and all the hounds of Cottesmore; and overhead rushed and whirled the skein of terrified wildfowl, screaming, piping, clacking, croaking, – filling the air with the hoarse rattle of their wings, while clear above all sounded the wild whistle of the curlew and the trumpet note of the great wild swan.

They are all gone now. No longer do the ruffs trample the sedge into a hard floor in their fighting rings, while the sober reeves stand round, admiring the tournament of their lovers, gay with ruffs and tippets, no two of them alike. Gone are ruffs and reeves, spoonbills, bitterns, avosets; the very snipe, one hears, disdains to breed. Gone, too, not only from the Fens, but from the whole world, is that most exquisite of butterflies – Lycaena dispar – the great copper; and many a curious insect more. Ah, well, at least we have wheat and mutton instead, and no more typhus and ague; and, it is hoped, no more brandydrinking and opiumeating; and children will live

and not die. For it was a hard place to live in the old Fen;
a place wherein one heard of 'unexampled instances of
longevity', for the same reason that one hears of them in
savage tribes – that few lived to old age at all, save those
iron constitutions which nothing could bleak down.
(Kingsley, *Prose Idylls, New and Old*, 1882)

It is hard for my country-bred grandchildren even to imagine
the flower-rich meadows of my own childhood, the clouds of
butterflies, the winter storms of migrating birds, rivers that
seemed always to be full of fish catchable with a hazel rod,
black cotton and a bent pin. Yet all the evidence shows that that
domain, paradisal to me in memory, was already very severely
poorer than that known to John Clare or Gilbert White at the
end of the 1700s, and that in turn much, much poorer than
the world Etheldreda knew.

Daniel Defoe's *A Tour Thro' the Whole Island of Great
Britain* (1724-1727) describes seeing what he thought was
a million swallows on the Suffolk coast. Bede, writing a
generation or so after Etheldreda died, describes Not-Yet-
England as rich in cattle and beasts of burden, land– and
waterfowl, and fish, including salmon and eels so common
that even the poor sometimes disdained them, surrounded
by seas teeming with dolphins, whales and seals. Eagles and
wolves and cranes were common. Place names from the period
recall the activity of beavers, and the presence of the noble and
dangerous wild boar. Otters left their spraint by most rivers.
The Fen would have been pulsating with life, its summer
air a cloud of insects and those who fed on them, its deep

brown pools the haunt of eels and frogs and the menace of the stockstill waiting heron, its slow rivers full of fish, even including sturgeon. You would have smelt on a hot day the odour that rises from summer grass and still water, with the occasional sulphurous whiff of rot as a bubble of marsh gas broke surface when a punt pole stirred the mud.

From the level fen, which you might have crossed afoot on one of the old trackways (but most likely you would have used a boat), the bulk of the Isle would dominate the northern or eastern view. As you landed, you would probably have passed stands of osiers at the water's edge, the yearly cropped 'rods' of which were made into baskets and cradles and fish traps and wattle for walls and so many other things: a key resource in the old economy, and so for many more centuries.

The view to the high land would have been a great deal more treed, for trees were husbanded carefully. From them came fuel, wood for building, and for making everything from farm tools to carts to stools. (And, in a hungry season, fodder for animals: for cattle love elm shoots and leaves, and acorns fatten pigs a treat.) Some trees that we take for granted were not there: no weeping willows by the banks trailing their long fingers in the water, for they did not come from China until the eighteenth century; no springtime fresh fire-coal chestnut falls loud with insects, for they came about the same time; no sycamores, for that messy and prolific tree only arrived after 1500; very few conifers.

There would have been smoke: smoke from cooking, of course, but also from brewing, even from metalworking and glass making – though that last had not really caught on much yet, despite evidence of it about 680 from Bede's monastery at Jarrow[22]. It would have been woodsmoke, or in the Fens the reek of peat. Get the wind right, and you would get the stink of the tannery. There would almost certainly be the lazy smoke of a limekiln somewhere, for lime was an essential material. A monastery, a community by definition, had to be self-sufficient: it was not all high thinking and devout rapture, but needed a whole web of interlocking physical support, hard and dirty work, and management. Someone had to dig the latrines and clean them out. (By the way, in default of paper, they seem to have used moss. Sphagnum is very absorbent.) And someone had to draw up the rotas.

What you would *not* have seen were the turning sails of the windmills that were so common later on the Isle. They only start to appear in England in the 1100s. The Romans had had watermills, driven by rivers, and we do know of a very, very few, manly sideshot, Saxon ones from the 7th century onwards, usually in connection with high status sites. And that is a clue to how hard, unremitting, was the daily work done simply in order to keep fed. Much grinding, essential to the making of daily bread, was done as it had been, time out of mind, piecemeal, with a quern, and there had been for centuries a trade from the parts of Britain where there was hard stone like millstone grit to the parts where the bedrock was chalk or a soft limestone. In this part of the world the nearest really hard stone was from Hertfordshire, a water-deposited silica-bonded conglomerate

---

[22] The two palm glasses in the young girl's grave in Ely (see page 61) were made, it is thought, in Kent.

called, delightfully, puddingstone – because it looks like a Christmas pudding with currants. Quite a few querns of this material have been found in and around Cambridgeshire and Ely, and much of the bread for any community would be made from grain ground in this way.

As you went up the slow slope from the Fen, you would have seen a cluster of low houses, perhaps (where the land drained well) what archaeologists like to call *grubenhauser* sunk a couple of feet into the ground. The walls would mostly be wattle – osier or split hazel woven between timber uprights – and daub – clay, cowhair and cowdung puddled to a plaster-like consistency. Sometimes the wall might be clay bats, which are clay puddled with straw, pressed into a mould, and dried in the sun into blocks the size of breeze blocks, and mortared together with lime mortar. Mud huts, in fact, and nothing wrong with that as long as you keep the weather out with a coat of limewash. I know several sixteenth and seventeenth century ones I could not get anywhere near affording, of which admiring people take photos and which are advertised in *Country Life*. From thatched roofs thin smoke would be rising.

Chimneys were some centuries in the future, and the old idea of the smoke from the fire on the hearth escaping through a hole in the roof has been challenged on the very good grounds that a through draught would make the fire burn too fast and create the risk of sparks setting the whole place alight. (Ancient and mediaeval villages and towns burned down with depressing regularity anyway.) What you wanted was a slow, steady heat. I have been in such a dwelling among the Sami of north Norway, where the smoke filters through the thatch, and you soon get used to the smokiness. Besides, it keeps down vermin and flies, and you can hang a ham in the rafters where it will keep beautifully, getting richer and richer. Houses would be darker than we might find comfortable, though, for windows, where they existed, were, as the Old Norse parent, *vindauga,* of the word says, 'wind eyes'. If the openings were closed at all, it would be with oiled parchment – sheepskin – which lets through only a little light. Shutters would blank light out completely.

You would have been wearing clothes of wool, often rather scratchy (think of Harris Tweed next to the skin!), or, if you were lucky and could afford it, lawn, fine plain weave fabric made from linen. Furs or leather might have protected you from cold or wet. Only the very wealthiest could afford the exotic silk, all of which had to cross Asia on caravans from China on the Silk Road to the markets of Syria and then Byzantium; only the richest could afford the fine cotton cloth from Mosul, muslin, for their ladies. Dyes would have been plant or earth based, or in the case of expensive red, made from crushed ladybirds. And all this fabric had to be spun by hand, using the oldest of tools, a distaff and a weight. It all had to be woven by hand. No woman from queen to churl was long without a distaff in her hand, unless she was doing some other task. (Hence the old phrase in family trees, 'on the distaff side.') And on your feet, shoes made of leather were often untanned and rarely waterproof, even if greased well with smelly tallow which you rendered down from the last sheep you killed.

You would probably be travelling, if you were wise, in the easy seasons of the year, when food and fodder were more plentiful and the blast of the bitter cold winters of that time had ceased. The hungry time came depressingly each year, when before the spring got going the stores laid up for winter were running out, the salted, dried and smoked fish and meat (if you could afford it) was scarce or going foul, and the fields were still bleak and wet and cold.

They called it the Hungry Gap. You could not, then, keep many animals over the winter for lack of winter fodder, and had to kill all but the breeding stock off and preserve them by salt or smoke at Martinmas: all that changed with the eighteenth century introduction of the swede turnip.

Before that you would have been happy to put the leaves of the plants that green up early, like ground elder, or nettles, or the roots of dandelion, or pig nut, hawthorn leaves or even the roots of reed mace and clover in your pottage with what remained of the oatmeal or barley or rye: and if that has gone mouldy you ran this risk of ergotism. You would have been very glad to find fish in the rivers and ponds to add to it.

But the hens will soon be laying, and you can harvest the eggs of wild birds and trap them with limed twigs, and one day the Spring will arrive. Pray there is not a late frost to blight the fruit blossom... Everyone, monasteries and courts included, went through this yearly cycle of feast and fast and weakness, and you can see why so much is made in northern European writing of the joys of spring and the privations of winter.

As you climbed up from the west you would have passed a graveyard: only a few graves so far, but one of them is clearly important, as it has a mound – a barrow – over it.[23] (The excavators remark that this cemetery 'may well have been associated with the first monastery in Ely.') Round the heart of the monastery, there would be a *vallum* – a ditch and rampart – not for any sort of defence but to mark where you were entering the special precincts – just as at Æbbe's Coldingham or Columba's Iona. Etheldreda's foundation[24] would have looked very like the sort of monastery she would have known at Æbbe's house, or Hild's 'Whitby', or Cuthbert's Lindisfarne: a collection of small huts (*casulae* or *domunculae*, 'little houses' or 'little dwellings', are the words often used, for example at Coldingham) for the individual monks and nuns – like Cuthbert's on Hobthrush Island, fifty yards offshore of Lindisfarne. This was the pattern the Desert Fathers and Mothers had adopted in Egypt at the dawn of monasticism.

There was perhaps a central hall for eating together and certainly a central church for worship. If so, those first community buildings would almost certainly have been wood, not stone[25], and probably impressive: the fairly modest

---

[23] The reports (*Antiquaries Journal*, 2009) of the excavation of the cemetery in West End, Ely, do suggest there might have been a mound over the richly furnished grave of a high status teenage girl: the exhibition in the Ely Museum was called 'The Grave of a Princess?'.

[24] Which was not where the cathedral and Norman monastery is, but somewhere to the west: nobody is quite sure where.

[25] One of the reasons Anglo-Saxon archaeology is so difficult is that especially in the earlier period they built mostly in wood, not stone, and wood rots and can leave few traces.

tenth century timber church of Greensted in Essex, or the huge royal hall at Sutton Courtenay, or the remains of Edwin's great palace at Yeavering in Northumberland, which Etheldreda must have known, indicate how sophisticated and richly dight a timber hall – like Hrothgar's Heorot in *Beowulf* – could be. (Theoden's Meduseld in the film of Tolkien's *Lord of the Rings* is not a bad impression.) In all probability the minster would have had a two-celled layout, with a sanctuary to the east. It would have had a bell, to call the community to prayer and worship.

We do not know what monastic rule her monastery followed. St Benedict's (he died in 547) wise *Rule* for living in community was not universally followed even as late as the monastic reforms of Archbishop Dunstan in the 10th century. At Ely, Bishop Æthelwold of Winchester, when he refounded the community in 970, insisted it abandon its previous constitution and discipline and become a men-only community of monks obeying the Benedictine rule. Unfortunately we have no record of what that abandoned discipline was, only of how the ladies and gentlemen of the house had got up to quite inappropriate high jinks – at least, that was what the reformers said: but then, they would, would they not?

Many founders of monastic communities – and so many of them were of noble rank and saw the monastery as a sort of family property to be kept among one's relations – devised their own rule. Sometimes these aristocratic communities might be more like a household, run with a focus on Christian life, and indeed aristocratic girls might be sent there for education. (One cannot help wondering whether the two young high status

girls in the cemetery were not in Ely for that very reason.)
Etheldreda's devoutness and asceticism, documented by Bede,
suggest that her pattern could have been quite a strict routine
of prayer and communal worship, work and personal discipline.
It is, I think, probable that with her connections to Wilfrid,
the chief proponent at the Synod of Whitby of obedience
to Rome, her rule for her Abbey may well have reflected his
thinking as well as having the practical examples of Æbbe's
and of the well-established Iona/Lindisfarne communities.

Which brings us to the issue of what a religious life was
all about.[26] Our culture treats the satisfaction of bodily needs
and desires as an obvious good, as paramount. It is simply has
no tools to understand what ascesis is about. Ascesis, severe
self-discipline and abstinence from the demands of the body
from food to sex, is a deliberate going into training just like an
athlete. The aim is to train the body to work in unison with the
mind to apprehend the shadows of the Divine as they appear
to mortal sense. For, so it was held, at the Fall, the mind/
body harmony was fatally dislocated, and appetite began its
despotic rule, even to the point where it overrides reason and
knowledge. St Paul expresses this mind/body clash perfectly in
Romans Ch. 7, vv. 19-25:

> *'I see another law in my members, warring against the law
> of my mind... For the good that I would, I do not: but the
> evil which I would not, that I do.'*

---

[26] Much of the following couple of pages summarises what I wrote in my *Crossroad:
A Pilgrimage of Unknowing* (Darton, Longman and Todd, 2022), pp.181ff.

Excess of food, far, far beyond what was – *is* – needed for survival, leads to unruly desires and uncontrollable impulses to sex, and anger, and covetousness and sloth. One of the reasons why sex was regarded by theologians with such uneasiness was that it was sexual desire for his wife that traditionally led Adam to cast God's injunction to the winds and sink his teeth into the apple[27] she offered. ('If you don't do this, you don't love me...') Deliberately to do without everything not absolutely necessary, aimed to bring body and desires back into proper subjection to the spirit. So fasting and watching, discipline and silence, chastity and frugality, were far from being ends in themselves. Far indeed from life-denying, these disciplines were a way to achieve a readiness for the Joy beyond the walls of this world which all desire, though they may know it not. The aim is to quieten the mind so that one can hear... 'Listen' is, after all, an anagram of 'silent'. For the whole object of the exercise is driven by love and desire: as the Psalm (84) puts it,

'My soul hath a desire and a longing to enter into the courts of the Lord, my heart and my flesh rejoice in the living God.'

Love lies at the heart of all: and, writing about 400, St Augustine – a man the effects of whose coruscating intellect reverberate even today in a world that mostly hardly knows of

---

[27] St Jerome's Latin version of the Bible uses the word *malum*, which is so often translated as 'apple'. But while *malus* (masculine) does denote the family of apple trees, *malum* (neuter) simply means 'evil'. Jerome was not above puns, of course. In parallel myths of fatal fruits, it's usually a pomegranate that is consumed. Given the climate, that is plausible.

him – has a wonderful passage in his *Confessions* which puts it better than I ever could (not surprising):

> *Late have I loved Thee, O Beauty so ancient and so new; late have I loved Thee! For behold Thou wert within me, and I outside; and I sought Thee outside and in my unloveliness fell upon those lovely things that Thou hast made. Thou wert with me and I was not with Thee. I was kept from Thee by those things, yet had they not been in Thee, they would not have been at all. Thou didst call and cry to me and break open my deafness: and Thou didst send forth Thy beams and shine upon me and chase away my blindness: Thou didst breathe fragrance upon me, and I drew in my breath and do now pant for Thee: I tasted Thee, and now hunger and thirst for Thee: Thou didst touch me, and I have burned for Thy peace.* (Book X, Ch. XXVII)

Jesus was always going alone into lonely places to pray to the Father. The 3rd and 4th century Desert Fathers and Mothers of Egypt, from whom the monastic life descends, imitated this. For them, ascesis was a mystical and unending search for ever greater closeness to the Divine – which indeed is often expressed through the metaphor of human sexuality, as in the way the *Song of Songs* was read, where the soul is enraptured by her lover, God.

For the early Irish church and its daughter churches in Iona, Melrose, Lindisfarne and so on, spiritual and bodily discipline was the necessary, enabling, complement to its daily nuts and bolts ministry among the people. (Even as communities, though, monks in the Irish tradition were pretty solitary, each one in his own little cell – rather like, much later, the austere Carthusians.)

People – not all Irish – like Molaise, or Columba, or Columbanus, or Aidan, or Cuthbert, or Guthlac, sought ever more remote, inhospitable places for their prayers and studies. All round the coasts of Ireland and Scotland and Wales you can find traces of little huts, often ingeniously built of dry stone in places where wood was not to be had. Not much bigger than a large dogkennel, these were the homes of these *athletae Christi*, 'Christ's athletes': the Greek means 'those who compete for a prize.' (Cf. Paul's 1 *Corinthians*, 9.24) On Iona one is still pointed out, a circle of fallen stone in about the loneliest spot in the island, where the wind keens in the heather of the moor, and the sound of the restless sea beyond the ancient hill fort the forgotten people made, to the west, underlines the isolation. Skellig Michael, off the Kerry shore, a tower of rock rising straight out of the sea with scarce land to feed a hen, was home to a small community of ascetics: in that wind they could hardly be anything else. They made little gardens for vegetables out of shattered limestone and rotted seaweed and protected them from the Atlantic gales with drystone walls.

St Ronan abandoned a successful life as a bishop in Brittany and took up his lonely station on North Rona, off the Butt of Lewis. His sister Brianhuil took herself off to the guano-covered wave-gnawed rock to North Rona's west, Sula Sgeir, over which the waves break in big storms. (I went there once, and saw it shining to the west as the dawn sun came above the horizon and lit its whiteness.) Later, they found her dead in a bothy there, her rib cage sheltering the nest of a shag. Cuthbert, leaving Aidan of

Iona's Lindisfarne – 'too comfortable' – meditated for years on the bleak, bird-noisy Farnes.

Just a little later than Etheldreda's founding of her double monastery, Guthlac, a Mercian noble, left the double monastery at Repton and went to the island of Crowland, just over the Fen from Ely, where he lived in the stone kist of a plundered barrow, eating only a piece of barley bread at sunset, and, like St Antony Abbot, in the Egyptian desert, plagued by demons.[28]

The people around these men, and some women, who turned all normal worldly values upside down, gave them huge authority[29]. The folk of Dal Riata and Ulster and the Islands constantly sought judgement and counsel from Columba and his successor Abbots of Iona. People from all over Northumbria constantly bothered Cuthbert for wisdom and guidance; they travelled from all over Strathclyde to seek out wise Molaise sitting in his cave under a rock overhang in the precipitous west side of Arran's Holy Island where a spring has its source. Guthlac's meditations were regularly disturbed by people seeking counsel, and the future king of Mercia, Æthelbald, took refuge with and counsel from him in his marshy fastness.

---

[28] There is an eighth century Latin *Vita Sancti Guthlaci*, by one Felix, which luridly describes the demons entering Guthlac's cell. Severe privation can lead to hallucination, as can bread infected with mycotoxins.

[29] In the Middle Ages the walled-in anchorite or anchoress in a humble church just down the road from you – like the wise lady we call Julian of Norwich – often had great importance and respect in the community, being consulted on all manner of issues and problems. A handbook for anchoresses written in the thirteenth century, the *Ancrene Riwle*, warns them against becoming centres of local news and gossip.

To us all this is weird. But our views would be equally weird to them, and there are many today who *do* keep alive this old rumour of the Other. Our culture has no words to talk about the supernatural save in computer games and fictions: but our forebears in any culture (and people in many today) would not have the faintest understanding of our easy, dismissive, dichotomy between Nature and Supernature. For them and for many across the globe now, supernature was everyday. Evidence of miracles was all round them, as it is round us. But we, trained as we are in the materialist West through the last four centuries either not to see it or explain it away, are blind to it. Nobody has proved our forebears wrong. And work at the frontiers of quantum physics is beginning to suggest that the reductive materialist model of the universe is not just bankrupt but, as long suspected, also plain wrong.

But though spiritual discipline and self-denial were (as exam rubrics used to say) 'To Be Attempted By All Candidates', monks and nuns did live in a community and had a duty of charity and hospitality to the people among whom they were set. The *Rule* of St Benedict (480-550) holds up an ideal of each day balanced between physical work (according to ability) and worship. It became dominant in western monasticism for 15 centuries, and is a thoughtful and practical guide for living in a community. It was certainly known to Wilfrid, and its 73 chapters have a good deal of advice for how the head of the community should rule it spiritually and practically. What do you do with an awkward monk or nun, for example...

Being an Abbess, or Abbot was not something to be taken lightly. What did it entail? Status: which is why so many were of noble or royal lineage. After all, a monastery or abbey was a big operation, a hierarchical community, a major economic player – and, later, often a major industrial site and economic engine. A monastery set up in a howling wilderness – as so many Cistercian ones were later – will, ironically, often turn that wilderness into a rich and productive estate.

But the model of a monastery to which we are accustomed was still in formation. In the early years many of them, as we saw, formed part of a family's patrimony *and* responsibility: many of the successors to Columba in Iona were his relatives, and Etheldreda was succeeded in Ely by her sister and nieces. (Indeed, a family religious foundation might also come in handy as a sort of retirement home for elderly relatives.

To run one you needed a good head for business, a usable network of contacts, and a flair for appointing the right people to subordinate positions – just like a modern CEO. You also needed, most important, the spiritual authority and charisma, and the understanding of and concern for people, to govern the community under your authority, many of whom would be equally as well born as you and just as intelligent.

But leadership is a lonely role. In an enclosed community, if you are sensible, you can have no real intimates, and to cope with that you need a great deal of spiritual strength and moral authority: which is why the traditional role of Bishop's Chaplain was once so important, as the one person to whom the Lord Bishop could unburden their fears and sorrows under the seal of confession.

Faith without works is dead... a duty of charity: clothe the naked, feed the hungry, comfort the dying, visit the sick... the monasteries did all those things. They were poor relief, hospitals, schools, builders of essential infrastructure like bridges (the Latin for priest, *pontifex*, means 'bridge builder' though that bridge is spiritual as well as physical). But Charity is about Love in action, and at the heart of the monastery's life was prayer and intercession for the world God loved into existence: and praise for the glory that was revealed in the risen Christ.

Entering a monastery was something done by many noble, indeed royal, women like Ælfred's daughter Æthelgifu. If rich enough, you might almost be *expected* to found one, as Æthelburh, sister of Erkenwald, Bishop of London, did at Barking just a few years before Etheldreda. (Like hers, it was a double monastery.) Not all of them were nice well-behaved ladies, let alone saints: we have already come across Cwenthrith.

To found such a community, you need land, and land is wealth and power. Etheldreda had land, good productive land, so one might say, in spades. Women with land and power, especially with the peculiar authority of the religious, had the clout to create alliances with the Church and influence secular rulers, as we saw with Hild or Æbbe. Abbesses of royal blood could act as intermediaries in political negotiations and so – let us not be too high-minded – might well usefully promote the political agendas of their own families. Their house could provide a neutral space where conflicting parties might meet on uncompromising ground. Etheldreda's creation of a well-financed monastic community at Ely certainly helped to bolster the authority of her secular family in East Anglia, who in turn could/would help support her community with further gifts.

But an abbess, like an abbot or CEO, had to ensure the house paid its way, and so arrange for the purchase or provision of essentials – like, to take just one example, the indispensable salt we take for granted, but which then was laboriously produced by boiling seawater, or by dangerous mining. Without it you could preserve nothing. What the monastery could not produce, it had to buy, and that meant money, and selling its own produce. The Head of House had to plan and facilitate building: granaries to store grain against each year's inevitable hungry season, accommodation for the community, support for maintaining the farms it owned, and at the heart of it all the incessant making of a place beautiful for God, and in its constant worship, to be a glimpse of Heaven. The pattern of that was Solomon's Temple, its ideal the New Jerusalem that St John saw in his vision.

It is difficult at this distance in time to get any clear grasp of how she discharged her role as Abbess in the seven years that were left to her after she came south again to Ely. It will not have been a rest cure – apart from anything else, the buildings had to go up even if there were some there already. It would have made sense to go to the buildings she had left when she had to go north, for one can assume that they would have been maintained in some sort.

Ely was after all an important place and had been so for a long time, on rich land, with a population then probably greater than Cambridge. (Only in the later fourteenth century, despite Ely being the seat of a major bishopric and administrative centre, did Cambridge overtake it in numbers.) The Roman road is proof that here was a Roman presence, and we can assume that in later Roman Britain there would have been a Christian presence which was probably extinguished by the Saxon arrival. Indeed, there is a curious passage in the twelfth century *Liber Eliensis* saying that on the island there had been a church founded by Augustine of Canterbury, but that it was destroyed by Penda.[30]

Etheldreda, it goes on, laboured to rebuild it and dedicated it to the Virgin Mary (*LE* i.15). Lots of deliberate symbolism there...

The earliest written record of her as Abbess is from Bede, writing some forty years after her death, when her reputation as a saint – which happened very quickly – was already gathering strength and will have influenced how people could look at her in her time. His account is certainly to some degree coloured by the fact that veneration of her remains is already well under way, but ought not to be dismissed as merely What One Says About A Saint. He mentions none of the things about her position that we would dearly like to know, simply because when he was writing everyone *did* know. So he concentrates on her self-denial and holiness.

---

[30] There is no record of Augustine working so far outside Kent and the Thames valley, and foundation by him is unlikely. But it was useful for the compiler of the *Liber* to stress the link between Ely and Canterbury, since his work is not history as we might understand the term, but the authorising myth of the community to which he belonged.

He describes her way of life there in terms intended to indicate that she strictly espoused monastic values as promoted by Pope Gregory the Great: which, for him, was the ideal, but may not have been her actual practice. He says she refused to wear anything but scratchy woollen – that is not uncommon, and a character in Shakespeare's *Love's Labours Lost* speaks of 'going woolward for penance.' At a time when many of her more affluent contemporaries took hot baths fairly regularly, she seldom washed in warm water, and had hot baths only at the great feasts of Easter, Whitsuntide and Epiphany. Even then she would only take a bath after everyone else had done. With her own hands, says Bede, she washed the 'handmaids of Christ' first. (Heating the water for a hot bath, carrying the water in pots to fill the large wooden bath tub, holding at least 100 gallons, was quite an operation, and not one to be taken lightly – for one thing, it used an enormous amount of fuel, all of which had to be cut and carted. By the time the Abbess got into the tub, the used water would have been pretty lukewarm – and grubby.[31])

Never except on the great feast days, or when ill, did she eat more than one meal a day. Unless ill, from Matins (the first of the seven canonical hours, while it was still deep dark) until dawn she would stay on her knees in the church in prayer. But of how she thought – she wrote nothing, though she was probably able to – and of the daily details of how she ruled the community, we know nothing. The fact that

---

[31] Basic soap was made with wood ash, lime and oil or tallow. You could add herbs – lavender, rosemary, for example – for scent.

her house survived and prospered, though, suggests she and her successors got a lot right, for, then and later, religious foundations did fail. Her moral influence was clearly soon felt: many of her friends and relatives followed her into the monastic life and many seem to have come to her for advice. That was perhaps to be expected. Some remained in Ely and the evidence of the cemetery, if it is indeed connected to the nunnery as seems probable, suggests that they perhaps entrusted their daughters to her care. But, of course, as a woman she could not administer the sacraments – a male priest had to do that – and her confessor at the monastery was probably one of the monks, called Huna, who helped her through death. (Later, he lived as a hermit near Chatteris, and died c. 690.)

Meanwhile, her faithful Ovin seems to have acted as her steward, bursar, and estate manager. Running a big estate, keeping the accounts (perhaps with tally sticks), planning the crops, arranging the sheepshearing and the carding of the wool for spinning, seeing to the needs for metalwork, simple things like nails, every single one hand-forged – not much time for the contemplative life there! I am glad his cross has been found and has an honoured place in the great Norman Cathedral that succeeded the fane he would have known, and for which he bought the hewn timber, and the lime and daub: and organised the men to build it.

The new community was as much at risk from disease as anywhere else in an age before all the things we take for granted. Of course, the early years were the most dangerous: if you made it to about 14, you had a reasonable chance of living to a good age, but at birth your chances were pretty low. The nuns and monks would certainly as a priority have planted a physic garden, for the arts of herbal healing were well developed and surprisingly effective. Willow bark tea for anything from headache to flu – it contains aspirin – or opium from poppies as an anaesthetic for really serious pain – well, when you are next in Ely walk round the physic garden at the east end of the Cathedral and enjoy learning about the qualities of those plants you thought you knew, or thought were weeds, and if you suffer from depression (who doesn't, to some degree?), St John's Wort is not just a pretty plant. Valium the tranquilliser gets its name from valerian, known as a sedative for untold centuries.

In fact, early medicine, while theoretically based on many false premises, may well have been more effective than we allow. For example, from the deserted mediaeval village of Wharram Percy on the Yorkshire Wolds, one twelfth century skull has been excavated showing that a successful trepanning had been carried out and the patient had recovered. This is a couple of centuries *before* any written text in the West describes that operation.

Even so, disease, from common coughs and cold – the Fens do them rather well – to the flea-borne plague, *yersinia pestis,* did happen regularly, and it is plausible that that it was plague that killed Etheldreda – Bede says it was *pestilentia,* but that could mean a number of nasty things. (On the other hand, it could have been a quinsy.) The community seems to have lost several of its members in the early years, if the cemetery you might have passed as you approached was indeed connected with it. It had some sixteen burials, male and female with a wide spread of age, contemporary with the very first period of the monastery. Two of them were of young women, one between 10 and 12, the other 15 to 17, and that of the younger, which was the more richly furnished, held a gold, silver and amethyst[32] necklace with a Tau cross pendant and two unbroken, beautiful, glass palm bowls. She was clearly Christian, clearly important, one can't help wondering who she was... a young noblewoman surplus to the requirement of marriage alliances between the great, parked, as so many were, in an aristocratic nunnery where she had a chance of a genuine if celibate career path?[33]

And then came death... Whose daughter, whose cousin, was she? She was important enough to have had that mound raised over her burial and there can have been few families at the time with the means to furnish her burial so richly, and they all knew, or were related to each other.

---

[32] Possibly significant: amethyst in Greek means 'not intoxicated' and was often used in episcopal rings as a mark of abstinence.

[33] It is so often not acknowledged that the mediaeval Church provided a genuine and serious career path for women. They could rise to positions of great economic and political power – and scholarship. (And if you think I am going to mention Hildegard of Bingen, you are right. But also Heloise – of Heloise and Abelard fame – Abbess of the Paraclete, Teresa of Avila, Herrad of Landsberg, Hild of Whitby...) Many nunneries were not strictly enclosed, and the women at Holy Trinity, Caen, for example, founded soon after the Conquest by Matilda, William's queen for her daughter Cecilia, were free to see their families, go regularly into Caen, and take part in city festivals and markets. Cecilia as Abbess was autonomous in a way her married sisters were not. She made all the decisions that governed her own life, she had authority over her community, and only answered to the bishop in Bayeux. For women could not, of course, administer the sacraments.

But her necklace reminds me of how Etheldreda, suffering from some sort of tumour below her jawbone (Bede says *tumorem maximum sub maxilla*) is said to have said it was penance for her taking too much delight in personal adornment, necklaces and things, when she was a girl. Bede reports that

> *she took great joy in this kind of sickness, and was wont to say, 'I know I most certainly do bear the burden of pain in my neck, on the which I remember, that when I was a girl, I did bear the superfluous burdens of necklaces: and I believe that the heavenly pity hath therefore willed me to be grieved with the pain in my neck, that so I may be acquitted from the guilt of superfluous vanity; whereas now instead of gold and pearls, the redness and burning breaketh out of my neck.'*

(Thomas Stapleton's translation, 1555)

That story goes on down the centuries, so that she became the saint whose intercession you sought for complaints of neck and throat, and, if a woman, for sore breasts. But more to the immediate point, the Harpole necklace, and the Ely jewels and necklace, and the 'ghost'[34] cross, as yet not fully excavated, at Harpole of which only fragments have so far been revealed, give

---

[34] An image can show up on X-ray before excavation, but when the soil is disturbed sometimes nothing remains. At Harpole, a large block of soil was lifted entire for micro-excavation. X-ray showed that the woman was buried with a large (30cm) and elaborate cross placed face down on her chest. See *Current Archaeology* 395 (2023) p.16.

us a very good idea of the sort of stunning, lavish jewellery she might have been remembering: for those remains are pretty well contemporary with her, and the extraordinary work in the some of the items in the Staffordshire Hoard shows that the skills and techniques continued to be practiced.

There was a certain Cynefrith, a *medicus* or physician, who was with her when she died, and when, as we shall see later, her body was exhumed. He said that he lanced the great swelling on her neck so that the noxious humour could be drained. (This is still a time – and will continue to be so for another 14 centuries – when medicine is based on balancing, 'tempering' or purging, the four fluids or humours in the body.)[35]

The lancing eased her, but the pain returned 'much more grievous' on the third day, and she died.

Her coffin, at her desire, was of plain wood, and she was buried, as she wished, at the heart of the community she had founded.

And the legend begins her rule from the tomb.

---

[35] The four humours (the idea goes back to Antiquity) are Blood, Melancholy or Black Bile, Phlegm and Choler. If these were out of balance, not tempered, their 'complexion' was 'distempered' and you could well have a temperature.

CHAPTER 4

Saint

What is a saint? Why do we need them? We use the word so loosely. When I was a child – before I was sensible enough to dismiss it – the image that used to come into the mind unbidden with the word was someone meek, gentle, forbearing, hands together, possibly with a half-heard aural wallpaper of Gregorian chant. Certainly humility, *real* humility, not that of the Uriah Heep kind, might be part of the job description: 'Not I, but Christ in me', says one of the all-time movers and shakers who had no false modesty, St Paul.

Humility is surely also a realistic recognition of what talents you have been given and what you have not, and a willingness to use them in selfless service. That is something so few of us ever manage. George Herbert says, as a preface to perhaps the finest devotional poems in our language, that they were 'a picture of the many spiritual Conflicts that have passed betwixt God and my Soul, before I could subject mine to the will of Jesus, my Master, in whose service I have now found perfect freedom.' The echo there of Cranmer's familiar Collect, echoing the opening of St Paul's letter to the Romans, 'in whose service is perfect freedom', blunts the force of the Latin *servus* or *servitium,* which would certainly have been in Herbert's mind. The words meant literal slavery, being a slave: giving up your will wholly to the will of another. But by contrast with secular slavery, this is not by constraint, but by a willing, rapturous casting it into the fire of Love that makes everything else seem weak and pale, an echo of harmony rather than the one equal music that holds all things in being.

This is, according to my reading, never without conflict and struggle. Many saints seem to have been reluctant to take on the implications of their surrender, which is at the same time overmastering desire. The saints of the Old Testament, the Hebrew prophets, were often afraid, struggling against the imperative to walk straight into grave danger, to make a nuisance of themselves and to speak uncomfortable truth to power and self-satisfied complacency in high places. That is one of the reasons we need saints, and prophets, men and women who remind people trapped in the wrong discourse, mindset, call it what you will, that there is a greater truth that must be acknowledged. It can cost not less than everything: I think of Bonhoeffer and the Nazis, or Becket and that able if choleric monarch Henry II. I think of St Francis, or St John Nepomuk, who refused to reveal the secrets of the confessional to his king, Wenceslaus IV of Bohemia. I think of Archbishop Romero gunned down by the assassination squad of the dictator of El Salvador – what an ironic name that country has! – as he was saying Mass in his cathedral; of Janani Luwum murdered by Idi Amin who could not bear the truth he was speaking. I think of men and women who give up everything we think matters to spend, in every sense, their lives in service to the poor and sick – like Father Damien of Molokai, working among the compulsorily quarantined lepers in Hawaii, caring for them in their abandoned reservation, organising building houses, schools, roads, hospitals, and churches. He dressed their ulcers, built a reservoir, made their coffins, dug their graves, shared pipes, and ate food with them, providing both medical and emotional support. And died of leprosy. And there are many saints who do not make it to the glamour of Wikipedia, but are unknown save to those to whom they have been a light shining in their darkness. They are needed in so many ways.

For more or less the last thousand years, in the (Roman) Catholic West, the process of declaring someone to be a saint has been by official and exhaustive examination of their life and works in a court, and the cause cannot be started without at least one report of a miracle resulting from invocation of the candidate.[36] The Devil's Advocate is appointed specifically to attack in every way possible the cause for canonisation. But (as

[36] In the Eastern Orthodox church spontaneous veneration of an individual by the faithful, accepted by the authority of a bishop, is the usual basis.

so often I have to say in this book) that had not happened yet. In the early Church there was no formal canonization, but cults of local martyrs – the word in Greek means simply 'witness' – were widespread, and regulated by the Bishop of the diocese. The translation of the martyr's remains from where they had been buried, to a church, was equivalent to canonization.

By the seventh century there is already a large list of saints with feast days in the calendar. In the Roman tradition especially, many of them do in fact go back to the years of persecution under the pagan Emperors such as Diocletian (284-305), when many Christians were indeed tortured and martyred in our usual sense. The stories told of them run to a pattern – the extraordinary fortitude of the martyr or saint, the certainty of a crown of glory – and a very early one, which becomes a paradigm, is that of Polycarp, Bishop of Smyrna in about 155, related by Irenaeus, also from Smyrna, who became bishop of Lyon later that century after the persecution by Marcus Aurelius. That setting up of a literary norm for the account of a saint becomes important for Etheldreda's story almost from its very beginning, soon after her death.

Her sister, Seaxburh, the devout queen of Kent, freed at last from the duties of regency when her son Ecgberht became king, moved to the new monastery as a nun very soon after its foundation. It cannot then have been wholly a place of hallowed peace, for there must still have been a lot of work going on.

Then Etheldreda died, and Seaxburh became Abbess, just as when she died in 699 her daughter Ermenhild, widow of

Wulfhere of Mercia, came back from being Abbess at Minster-in-Sheppey to succeed her in the family patrimony. Those Angles and Saxons certainly knew how to keep things in the family.

Hundreds of noble women had entered upon the religious life in Anglo-Saxon England, and they are now footnotes in unread books. But Etheldreda's shrine and Etheldreda herself rapidly became a major figure within the English religious landscape. And it is to Seaxburh that much of that is due. A determined woman of proven administrative ability – the 12th century *Liber Eliensis* described her as *pretiosa virago*, 'a precious heroic woman' (after all, she had run a kingdom) – during her abbacy it is clear she encouraged, and managed, the veneration of Etheldreda's grave that had had already begun to grow, and fostered her widening reputation as a saint. It was said, for example – Bede is our earliest witness – that Etheldreda had had the gift of prophecy, and had foretold her own death. It was decided – and Seaxburh as Abbess had to be behind this – in 695 that her remains should be exhumed and reburied in the church building, but in something more elaborate than a simple wooden coffin.[37] Which means stone, of which Ely has none, the nearest quarries of hard stone being miles away across the Fen. So Seaxburh

---

[37] This may also mark the beginning of a change in social assumptions and conventions about burial. It has been argued that in the pagan period prominent grave mounds, especially in clusters like at Sutton Hoo, were a family's or dynasty's way of making a massive statement of power and ownership. But then more important becomes being included in the Body of Christ, and increasingly we find that burial actually *inside* the church become a marker of secular power and status. And, indeed, remained so, long after the Reformation.

... bade certain of the brethren to seek a stone whereof they might make a coffin for this purpose; and they taking ship... to a little city left deserted, the which was not far from thence, which, in the language of the English, is called Grantacaestir, and by and by they found by the walls of the town a coffin of white marble, most beautifully wrought, and covered also very trim with a lid of like stone. Wherefore understanding that the Lord had prospered their journey, they returned thanks to Him, and carried it to the monastery.

(Bede, IV.19)

Bede's 'Grantacaestir' is not the place famous for having a church clock that, according to the poem, only tells the right time twice a day, but the important Roman station, Durolipons, on the bluff guarding where the via Devana from Colchester to Chester crossed the river we now call the Cam.

What the monks found was clearly a highly decorated sarcophagus, obviously once a very expensive import from a warmer climate for someone important. Its weight must have been getting on for half a ton: a plain limestone one, also Roman, found near Stuntney (just across the Fen from the modern cathedral) when a farmer's plough struck it, weighed about that. I imagine those monks manhandling it down to the river on rollers, into the boat, and then their journey down the meandering Cam to join the then much bigger Ouse, and finally, the huge labour of getting it across the Fen to the Isle and up the steep slope to the church: for the river then did not run close to the Isle, but close to the bluff of Stuntney.[38]

The exhumation was not something to be taken lightly. It was carefully planned to give a proper solemnity to the occasion. The community set up a tent over her grave while the digging was going on, and stood outside singing psalms. The ceremony of her translation had clearly been thought out carefully – by her sister? – and there were precedents for how it should be managed. (This had already happened with some of Etheldreda's kin, Æthelburh and a niece, between 660 and 670 at Faremoutiers-en-Brie.) Bishop Wilfrid, Ethedreda's friend, who had come down for the occasion, Seaxburh and others, went in to take up and wash the bones, when suddenly those outside heard a loud cry, 'Glory be to the Name of the Lord!' The body was found to be undecayed. Even the graveclothes were still intact. In Britain, (St) Oswald of Northumbria's arm, kept uncorrupted at Bamburgh, was already venerated, but what happened at Ely that October day was the first instance of an entire body being uncorrupted. (St Cuthbert was so found in 698). The impact of this miracle was immense.

Her physician Cynefrith, who had lanced her swelling, was there, and Bede quotes his account at length in direct speech – even to Cynefrith seeing the mark of his incision, which

---

[38] It was the Normans who diverted the river: probably to make it easier to bring in the vast quantities of stone needed for the cathedral. Wetting the clay would make a laden sled move more easily – as was done in quarrying chalk or clunch in this part of the world, just as the Vikings doing a portage would put wet seaweed under the keel of their boat.

had healed. (Bede could certainly have met and spoken to Cynefrith: and he did do his homework.) Incorruptibility of the flesh was taken as one of the diagnostics of sainthood. The nuns washed the body and put fresh clothes on it, and then placed it in the sarcophagus, which it fitted perfectly, even to the head fitting the space cut for the original owner.[39] Etheldreda was then translated into the church building where a shrine was later erected. Bede says that miraculous cures happened even to people who prayed by and touched the wood of her old coffin.

A brief digression: we had better think a little about relics before we go further, as there are/were quite a lot connected with Etheldreda. It's so easy to sneer at the credulity, the gullibility, of those who were so much less clever than we are (they were not, as a matter of fact). Certainly there were frauds about with bogus ones, like Chaucer's Pardoner in the *Canterbury Tales,* who relied on being able to dupe the trusting and unsuspicious. There were bogus relics held solemnly and reverently in churches. The bones of the supposed Holy Innocent the priests in the brief reign of Mary 1 installed in Durham Cathedral were beside the certainly genuine relics of St Cuthbert and St Oswald, but were those of a greyhound. Moreover, we clever moderns have a cult of relics every bit as pervasive as anything the Middle Ages knew, for it is a natural human need born of love and honour. 'That was

[39] Bede actually used both the word *locellus*, 'casket' when the monks first find the receptacle, and later *sarcophagus* when the body was placed therein. It has been argued, to my mind unconvincingly, that the object was more like a reliquary than a coffin. Size matters: you cannot put a body in a reliquary.

my mother's vase, that was...' Princess Diana's dresses draw thousands of visitors; Tolkien's old Oxford MA gown made silly money when sold at auction; memorabilia of the Beatles, letters written by the famous, give auctioneers a good living. I plead guilty too, for the lead that our beloved black Labrador Hector used still hangs, with a slip chain collar, on the hook by the back door even though he who used it is now a warm memory. That dog lead is as much a relic as the fragments of bone or cloth to which people made devout and arduous pilgrimage. But where it differs is that relics of something or someone holy introduce another dimension: the possibility of something spreading out from it with power and healing if you are ready to receive it. Why do we not use the Polynesian word and say they are conduits of *mana*, the force that holds the universe in being? After the Second Council of Nicaea in 787 it was made obligatory that any newly, consecrated church should have a relic in its altar.[40]

Having got that digression out of the way... In the whole of Bede's very long *Ecclesiastical History of the English People* there is only one poem – even of Caedmon's hymn of Creation, the importance of which he does recognise, he gives only 'the sense' in a Latin summary. He wrote 27 elegant Latin elegiac couplets immediately after his account of Etheldreda, which indicates how by 731, when he finished the book and included the poem, she was being accorded very high status as a saint

---

[40] A thoughtful essay I found illuminating about the sort of mindset that our forebears might have had about the sacredness of the body: Matteo Salonia, '*The Body in Medieval Spirituality: A Rationale for Pilgrimage and the Veneration of Relics*', *Interdisciplinary Journal of Research on Religion*, 14 (2018).

indeed. The couplets are 'serpentine': that is, in each couplet the end of each second line repeats the first three words of each first, and the 27 couplets are alphabetic. (There is neither 'w' nor 'k' in the Latin alphabet, hard 'c' doing duty for the latter sound and the place where we would expect the 'w' couplet is filled by an exclamation to Christ, 'this was thine own work', at the point in the poem when Bede describes the taking up of the uncorrupt body.) The last four couplets acrostically spell 'AMEN'.

Bede begins by rejecting as a subject the old heroic tales that so many schoolboys had read, admired (one hopes) and imitated: no repeating of Virgil's epic story of heroic Aeneas and his wars here, or the carrying off of 'tainted' (*foedae*) Helen of Troy and the fall of that city: 'My poem is chaste... I shall speak of heavenly gifts.' He immediately moves to the Incarnation of Christ through a virgin mother, and then moves on to list a number of key virgin saints and martyrs: Agatha (Sicilian, martyred under Decius), Eulalia (Spanish, under Diocletian), Tecla (her story is in the lovely but apochryphal *Acts of Paul and Thecla*), Euphemia (Bithynian – which is now Turkey – and Diocletian, again), Agnes (Roman, Diocletian) and Cecilia (Roman, under Alexander Severus).

This list of holy virgins makes an impressive build-up to the picture of Etheldreda's nobility, chastity, the incorruption of her earthly body which for Bede, as he says in his narrative of her translation, is a mark of her being *a uiri contactu incorrupta*, 'uncorrupted by the touch of a man', and her consequent powers against the Serpent that beguiled Eve. There is more than a hint of her being second only in importance to the Blessed Virgin Mary: a theme which becomes increasingly noticeable in her legend as her cult develops. Bede was clearly very impressed by her and in the world chronicle which he appended to his great treatise on time *De Ratione Temporum* (725)[41] he commemorated her together with Cuthbert, and, uniquely among English saints, gives her a full historical notice.

You do not look for the details of biography and background in a Saint's Life. That is not what the highly stylised genre does – and in terms of volume it is perhaps one of the most important kinds of narrative writing in the Middle Ages.[42] The Saint's Life is concerned to illustrate the fortitude and constancy of the saint in the face of awful and sometimes improbable torment and difficulty, the grace of God shown through them, and their continued power through the miracles attributed to them after intercession for their help. As far as details of the life, appearance, social context, how they thought – forget it. But as edifying material, filling out and encouraging devotion to the shrine and relics of a saint, they are as efficiently functional

---

[41] To Bede we in the West owe the convention of dating *Anno Domini*, from the birth of Christ. Older methods were direly difficult, by indictions or by regnal years (Acts of Parliament still are by the latter). He was not quite the first to think of it, though: that was a Greek monk, Dionysus Exiguus, ('Tiny Denis'). Indictions, as it happens, are fiscal periods of fifteen years and were used to date events and transactions in the Roman Empire and in the papal and some royal courts. The system was instituted by Constantine in 313 and was used in some places until the sixteenth century.

[42] And given the familiarity most people at all levels of society would have had with such writing, it gives a useful clue into how they thought about – constructed is I think the fashionable term – their world and their lives and experience.

as advertising. The real person, the princess and abbess, the woman who ate and drank and laughed and cried and was fierce and was gentle, who undoubtedly existed, is accreted to a norm of sanctity, and we cannot glimpse her.

A Saint's Life needs miracles, and many, improbably or not, were attributed to her. For example:

> *Ecgfrith ordered his men to get Etheldreda back. On the first day they nearly caught the fugitives, but they hid on the promontory of St Abb's Head. Suddenly a strong tide appeared which cut the promontory off the coast, barring the pursuers' way. Ecgfrith waited for the water to go down, but it did not, for seven whole days. Etheldreda and her companions spent all that time in prayer. Then at last did Ecgfrith understand that the Lord Himself was helping Etheldreda, and that it was His will that she be among holy nuns; so he stopped pursuing her and agreed to annul their marriage.*
>
> *During the journey south they were thirsty, she prayed, and a holy spring gushed forth by her feet.*
>
> *One very hot day Etheldreda felt very exhausted. There was no shelter from the sun. The saint stuck her staff in the ground and lay down. When she woke the staff had turned into a mighty ash tree in full leaf. (This legend is associated with Stow, in Lincolnshire, near where she is supposed to have crossed the Humber.)*

A lot of people wrote about Etheldreda in this hagiographic tradition, and the more it is done the more it flourishes. More medieval *Vitae* exist for Etheldreda than any other English female saint. Aelfric, Abbot of Eynsham, wrote about her (relying entirely on Bede), in the late tenth century. Goscelin of St Bertin composed *Vitae* of several female English saints, including Etheldreda, in 1082. There were accounts of her in Old and Middle English, in Latin, even Old French. Those accounts of her in the people's vernacular indicate that her sanctity, as something to be emulated and supplicated, was made repeatedly familiar to lay audiences.

Apart from all this, she appears in the annals – literally, the 'year story' e.g. 'In this year the cat died, in this year the Danes came with great havoc' – of several houses; she appears in chronicles and early calendars which mark her saint's day. Hers are 23rd June (her death) and 17th October (the translation of her body into the Abbey Church). The twelfth century *Liber Eliensis*, the 'Book of Ely', has a lot to say about her, but as the validating chronicle of Ely monastery (and by then Cathedral) it would, would it not? since the main claim to property the foundation owned is through and from her, and her cult is of immense value and prestige to the monastery. Indeed, her cult remained a focal point of worship in England throughout the Middle Ages.

From its very beginning she was elevated to a status far beyond that of your usual common or garden saint. That she was regarded almost as an English equivalent of the Blessed Virgin Mary herself is supported by the pose in a gorgeous full page miniature in the 10th century *Benedictional of St Æthelwold*, in the British Library, which shows her holding a book and the lily of chastity, with crown and crozier – her usual identifying attributes. Behind her is the legend in gold which reads: '*Imago s[an]c[t]e Apeldrype abb[atisse] ac perpetue virgin[is]*' – 'a picture of holy Athelthrythe the abbess and perpetual virgin'. Perpetual virginity is one of the attributes of Mary, and the phrase's use in the illumination is extraordinarily revealing. Moreover, the blessing in the book for her feast day, which may be by Æthelwold himself, prays that the Grace of God may 'remove from you all provocative concupiscence and ignite in you the fire of his love.'

Etheldreda's cult was developed rapidly in eighth-century Ely. The relics of the unperished body, placed apparently in a shrine near the main altar, her original grave clothes, and her coffin were venerated, and many pilgrims claimed that they had been cured of ills to do with eyesight and throat trouble. The growing tide of pilgrims brought offerings to the shrine, and the wealth of the community grew.

The cult was soon very valuable. Let us not be too cynical about this: that money enabled not only the building and making of beautiful things to honour the unspeakable glory of God, but also hospitals, poor relief – the poor were fed once a day at the gate of most monasteries – bridge-building, road maintenance, schools – and scholarship, thought and research, of which we, though we acknowledge it not, are only the latest beneficiaries. And quite apart from that: we have made ourselves a culture where trust is for fools and where everyone is so busy looking for the muddy trail of feet of clay that we have forgotten that there are such things as ideals by which people do try to live. With that depressing outlook, it is so easy to attribute stupid gullibility to the devout, and cynical manipulation to the managers – who of course are *far* too clever (like us) to believe what they are peddling. Everything I read, and know, of people, gives that the lie. Rogues and fools, cheats and liars there were, and are, and always will be. But those churchmen who managed the cults were cut from the same cloth as the pilgrims, lived in the same thought world, held the same values, feared and hoped for the same things. I am convinced that most of them believed in what they were doing. 'God has given us by His Grace a saint in our midst, who is herself a channel of His Grace. Let us do her honour and rejoice': that seems far more likely to be the attitude than 'In what new ways can we rip off these poor suckers?'

The cult spread: after Seaxburh died and her daughter Eormenhild (ex-queen of Mercia) became Abbess, the community seems to have been drawn into Mercia's sphere of influence and it was about then that Etheldreda was first promoted in the former kingdom of Lindsey, centred on Lincoln. Lindsey had for long been a pawn between Mercia and Northumbria, but by the 700s it was under Mercian control. The *Liber Eliensis* associates Etheldreda's cult with the foundation of two churches in Lindsey, and, indeed, there are still two churches with very early dedications to her, one at West Halton – near the crossing point of the Humber – and the other, a lovely mix of Saxon and Norman, at Stow Minster (later rededicated to St Mary).

At Ely, her mixed community of priests and nuns seems to have flourished for about two centuries. But in 793 the first of the Viking raids shocked the English and Frankish communities by the raiding and burning of Lindisfarne. Alcuin of York at the court of Charlemagne sees it as the beginning of Apocalypse. These raiders knew exactly what they were looking for, and they knew where to go: for had not many of them been coming to Eastern Britain for many years as traders? (Trade links with Scandinavia and Denmark are very ancient.) They wanted easily portable valuables: gold, silver, jewels, whatever damage it caused. But though pagans, they were not savages: they were good businessmen, who knew the market for relics. Pagan though they were, they recognised how much they could raise by selling raided relics in their expensive reliquaries to other churches who would pay well for them.

Times were tough and getting tougher back in Scandinavia. You had to pay your followers somehow, and the price of goods was going up worldwide. So in 865 all the smaller bands of Vikings got themselves organised and coalesced into what the *Anglo Saxon Chronicle* calls the Great Heathen Army. Now they did not go home for the winter, but stayed, basing themselves at Torksey near Lincoln. Why waste time and energy going home?

In 870 the Danes came in force to the Fenland. They attacked and burned Soham Abbey, founded by St Felix and resting place of his relics. The smoke and flames would have been seen from Ely's comparative eminence, a warning of what was soon to come. The Danes moved on to Ely, burned the buildings, and killed a lot of the community. But despite attempts to loot it, the shrine survived despite stories of one man trying to hack his way through its marble with his battle axe. (What a waste of a good axe!) In fact, the Danish sack had very little long term impact on the cult of Etheldreda.

Members of the community who had fled seem soon to have come back to Ely. By the 940s a community of married priests was again actively promoting Etheldreda.

But the times were changing, and reform was afoot. The hugely talented and very able Dunstan became Archbishop of Canterbury in 960, and engineered the appointment of Æthelwold, Abbot of Abingdon, to the very important See of Winchester. With his help, and with the ready support of King Edgar the Peaceful, Dunstan pushed forward major reforms in the English Church. No more married priests, their families comfortably inheriting or living off the revenues of church or shrine, no more lax discipline. Following this programme, Æthelwold refounded the monastery of Ely around 970 – which is why his *Benedictional* in the British Library has that great painting of Etheldreda.

The break with the past was complete: even his new church was not where the original one had stood. That is thought to have been more to the west, perhaps on the highest part of Ely's hill. Some suggest, plausibly, that it appropriated a site already sacred (perhaps even from pre-Christian times), near a spring. The site of Æthelwold's building is now covered by the present cathedral. The community now became wholly male and strictly Benedictine. Of course, there had to be a certain PR element in this reform, and the new monks' predecessors had to be excoriated as lax, unchaste, lazy and all the other things a good monk should not be. They were probably, like most of us, a mixed bag. But Æthelwold was certainly enlisting in the service of reform the seventh-century church, idealized by Bede, as a golden age of monasticism, with a plethora of serious saints, and that certainly was furthered by fresh sponsorship of Etheldreda's cult, as she was a model of what a religious example should be. The Benedictine monks duly recorded the saint's recent miracles, above all her punishment of their polluted predecessors.

The virginal and uncorrupted Etheldreda was a perfect symbol of the ejection of unchaste priests from Ely in favour of celibate Benedictines, and her inviolate and uncorrupted body was a perfect metaphor for the endurance of the monastery through Viking raids. But this posed something of a problem for Æthelwold and the new community. It was usual to display a saint's relics so they could be seen and reverenced by pilgrims. But removing the saint from her sarcophagus centuries after she had been put in it to put her remains on display might have risked shattering her reputation as incorrupt if they had decayed. So Æthelwold made the sarcophagus itself the focal point of her shrine. There was an elaborate ceremony when it was brought into its new position beside the high altar. Next to it were set the newly translated remains of Seaxburh and Eormenhild, together with those of another incorrupt virgin saint, Wihtburh – who just may have been another sister of Etheldreda (Bede does not mention her) – whose body the Ely monks stole from the monastery at Dereham in Norfolk: there is an account of the monks going relic-raiding in the *Liber Eliensis*[43] After all, stealing relics was not that uncommon,

---

[43] The chronicler (who claimed both King Edgar and Bishop Aethelwold had approved it) describes the raid, led by Abbot Brithnoth himself, as 'a holy sacrilege and a religious theft' justifiable because at Ely the relics would receive greater veneration and honour than at Dereham.

for relics brought pilgrims. (The biggest mass raid for relics was when the 4th Crusade, in hock to the Venetians – who themselves had stolen St Mark's relics from Alexandria – and needing to pay them, deplorably sacked the Christian city of Constantinople in 1204, resulting in a flood of relics to the West) This collection of four royal women associated with saintliness and incorruption was bound to be quite a draw. The abbot had gold and silver jewel-encrusted statues made of them to stand beside the high altar.

It was probably about then that stories, the sort of urban myth that you are told by someone who knew someone who was there, began to be told, warning of the dire consequences of trying to open the tomb. The *Liber Eliensis*, obviously using earlier sources, says that the Danish raider who ruined a good axe making a small hole into the tomb went blind and then dropped dead. When the priests who had fled the Vikings returned, one of them tried to poke the body through the hole with a fennel stalk, to see if it remained incorrupt. Finding that it was, he then attached a lit candle to a stick and poked this inside to see better, but immediately lost his sight. In the next few days, the story continues, his whole family died of plague...

And then... William the Bastard's shock victory – it was, as was said at another pivotal battle, 'a damned close-run thing' – at Hastings in 1066 changed everything. This was worse than anything the Great Heathen Army had done when it drove Ælfred to seek refuge in the marshes of Somerset. William's was in fact the last serious Viking invasion, for the Normans were Northmen, mainly from Norway, who had carved themselves a goodly slice of the fat land of what we now call Normandy out of the sweet land of Francia. Saxons were turfed off the farms their families had held since Etheldreda's folk came centuries before. Saxon churchmen were deprived of their livings, the North was drenched in blood, and when the smoke of its burning cleared, it was a silent land without cry of child or lowing of cattle.

William and his gang – most English people today, actually, will be descended from them as well as from their victims – were resisted. The most serious resisters eventually came together in the Isle of Ely surrounded by its fens and rivers and meres. Some of the northern earls joined with the legendary Hereward[44], and made common if unreliable cause with the Danes who also had a claim to the English throne. Morcar, earl of Northumbria, and others, including a large Danish force under Svein II, joined the group, secure in the protection of the Fens, raiding the land beyond their watery defences to get supplies. (However much you might resent William's conquest, it can't have been much fun being a Saxon peasant being raided, and Hereward himself, despite Kingsley's picture of him as a noble hero, was not above a bit of looting in addition.)

Etheldreda as saint now is given a new role: a symbol of resistance and of protection, a queen just as royal and much more holy than any Norman pretender. Rebels who joined Hereward had to swear an oath to the cause on her sarcophagus. The *Liber Eliensis* records miracles

---

[44] He was a nobleman, mentioned both in the eleventh century Peterborough continuation of the *Anglo Saxon Chronicle* and in the *Liber Eliensis*. The *Gesta Herewardi* was written quite soon after the rebellion.

demonstrating that she continued as protectress in this role in the decades after the Conquest. One story in particular makes her not only a protector of Ely, but also an avenger of unjust rule, supported by her sisters.

A Norman noble called Gervase treated the people of Ely very harshly, killing or imprisoning anyone who protested. But one night as he lay sleeping in the hall with his household, the saint appeared to him in a vision. This was by no means just the common male nightmare of being told off by an angry woman who won't let you get in a word in your defence. She held her crozier, symbol of her authority, and with her were Seaxburh and Wihtburh in support. In high passion she gave him the roughest side of her tongue:

'Are you the man who has been holding me in contempt and so often harassing my people – the people whose protectress I am? And have you not yet desisted from disturbing the peace of my church? What you shall have, then, as your reward is this: that others shall learn through you not to harass the household of Christ.' And she lifted the crozier she was carrying and drove its point heavily into the area of his heart, as if to pierce him through. Then her sisters, St Wihtburh and St Seaxburh wounded him with the hard points of their own staves. Gervase, with his fearful groaning and horrible screaming, disturbed the whole of his household as they lay round about him: all could hear him groaning, 'Lady, have mercy! Lady, have mercy!' His servants came running to see what the matter was. There was a noise round about Gervase

as he lay there and he said, 'Can't you see St Etheldreda going away? How she pierced my chest with the sharp end of her staff, and her saintly sisters did the same? And look, once more she is coming back to stab me, and now I shall indeed die.' And with that, he died.

William had indeed a tough job subduing the fierce resistance to his conquest that had concentrated in the Isle. He tried to build a wicker causeway across the marsh at Aldreth, but it collapsed or capsized more than once, drowning a lot of his men. Eventually, he made it: the Danes agreed to go home with a decent money payment in their scrips – they had got used to that profitable sort of thing under Æthelred the Ill-Counselled – and when the Abbot and the monks realised William was prepared to sit down for a long siege, they submitted.[45] William visited, and venerated the shrine of Etheldreda. The rebels – or should we call them freedom fighters? – either made a peace they could never trust, or melted away. The Normans piled up the huge Motte overlooking the monastery with a timber castle on its top to signal their control. The castle has gone, but the motte remains, a reminder of so many unhappy things in human history, but now a place where people walk their happy dogs and the worst missile is a ball thrown for their excited chase.

---

[45] And were fined the enormous sum of 1000 marks (£666.13.4). The last Saxon abbot was Thurstan (*ob.* 1072), a man of great learning, who was born and educated in the Isle of Ely. He was a boy at the predecessor of The King's School. He was appointed by King Harold Godwinson, but survived William to die peacefully.

But: despite the sainted ladies having been made into symbols for resistance against Norman oppression, the Norman abbots William appointed, and their successors, were keen to keep Etheldreda's cult flourishing. The Norman abbots set about a major rebuilding of Æthelwold's church as befitted the resting place in her palatine jurisdiction of the queen and saint who had founded their house. They were thinking on a very big scale indeed: some authorities think that Æthelwold's building would have fitted into the Norman nave, and was demolished piecemeal as the building went on. The nave is longer than Canterbury's and Salisbury's. That being the only part of the building into which lay people were allowed – for they could not enter the monks' part at all – suggests that a huge number of future pilgrims processing round it was anticipated. (To put things in a sort of perspective, someone calculated a few years ago that the cost of building a major twelfth century cathedral as a proportion of GDP was greater than the entire NASA space programme.)

The Crown also made the Abbey into a Cathedral, the seat of a Bishop who was a vassal of the Crown and thus a major political player, while the head of the monastery became a Prior. In 1106 the rebuilt choir was ready for the relics of the four women, which were moved to new shrines with Etheldreda in the position of honour east of the high altar. In the late eleventh and early twelfth centuries there were many more things written, in prose and verse, about her and her miracles, especially in the time of Ely's first bishop, Hervey (1109–31). (It is he who is believed to have commissioned the *Liber Eliensis*.) The great Marie de France, a fine and subtle poet about whom we know so regrettably little, wrote a verse version of her life, *La Vie Sainte Audrée*, in Anglo-Norman around 1200, and the flow continues right down to recusant Ralph (or Robert) Buckland's *Lives of Women Saints of our Contrie of England* (1610-15). Moreover, as Eamon Duffy has pointed out, the number of visual representations of a saint, in paint, in stone, in wood and so on, is a good indicator of popularity and devotion. After all, such things cost money, and nobody is going to make them just for fun.[46] The picture of Etheldreda – like the one on the front of this book, from North Tuddenham, Norfolk – appears on many rood screens that survive out of the hundreds that were lost at the Reformation. She is clearly recognisable by the lay people, who would have heard her *vita* in one form or another, by the Benedictine habit the Benedictine Æthelwold anachronistically gave her, and by her crozier and her crown.

The cult continued at Ely throughout the Middle Ages. So popular had Etheldreda become that besides Ely, some dozen medieval churches were dedicated to the saint. By the later Middle Ages her relics – objects connected with her – were widely distributed among English churches, including Glastonbury, St Albans, Salisbury, Thetford, and Waltham. Durham claimed to possess a stole she had given to St Wilfrid and in 1536 an East Anglian religious foundation allegedly

---

[46] There is an interesting discussion, with a list of surviving material and where it is, in Virginia Blanton-Whetsell, '*Imagines Ætheldredae*: Mapping Hagiographic Representations of Abbatial Power and Religious Patronage', *Studies in Iconography 23* (2002), pp.55-107.

held various personal items including a wimple and a comb. She had devotees in France and in Scandinavia. Success – is that the right word? – breeds success, and it generated more and more pilgrims, who needed more and more accommodation and infrastructure, and who brought more and more income.

Pilgrims, then as now, need souvenirs, preferably blessed at the shrine and having been in contact with it, and, as in many other holy places, there was a ready sale of little lead badges, like the 'We've been to [fill in as desired]' stickers some people used to stick on their car's windows. In Ely these were made in their hundreds, and depict, rather crudely, Etheldreda with her crown and crozier. Moreover, given her connection with diseases of the throat, it is no surprise that at the fairs at the season of her feast days lace collars and trimmings that had touched the shrine were sold. (Her name, spoken rapidly, wore down to 'Audrey', hence 'tawdry lace' – and 'tawdry' according to OED had no negative connotation before the seventeenth century.)

Inns and hostels did a good trade. Managing the numbers – especially on festivals – as they filed in, passed the shrine, made their supplications, often tearfully, and keeping the column moving – well, we all have experienced something not unlike it, but probably much less of a crush and much less smelly, at major exhibitions in museums like the British Museum. (Where we are pilgrims to a different sort of relic…?) There is also a striking similarity to the Queue that marked Her Late Majesty's Lying in State. You have got to keep the column moving in one direction, and here an ambulatory is a great help. The present one at Ely, which Bishop Hugh of

Northwold's extension of the choir eastwards made possible, must have been preceded by something similar, if not as small as the tiny one clockwise round the shrine at the Saxon church at Brixworth. But it is not just a question of dealing with people *en masse*: there are also individual pastoral needs to be met, and here the availability and readiness of individual priests to hear confessions, offer healing and counsel, and so on, must have continued to stretch the management's resources. So great were the numbers that the lovely and capacious Galilee porch of around 1200 may well have been built partly to allow pilgrims to gather prior to entering, to wash their feet after the dirt of their journey. (There are benches along the wall for the elderly and infirm – hence 'the weakest goes to the wall') Porches in some major churches did have their floors slightly sloping so that the water from any washing would drain out. The huge three bay westward section of Vézélay, which claimed in the twelfth century to hold relics of St Mary Magdalene, indicates the numbers a major shrine would expect.

Why these numbers? Going on a pilgrimage in the Middle Ages was something almost everybody did at some point in their lives, and sometimes several times. (There was a certain advantage in doing so if you had a lawsuit against you pending, say for debt, for all such legal proceedings were suspended while you were away.) Sometimes a pilgrimage might be quite modest, like going to venerate the relics held in a church in the next village, but the Christian geography of Europe was netted by long distance pilgrim routes to holy sites. It was a geography of stories of the saints and of the riches they had amassed in the Treasury of Grace which could help poor pilgrims, who were trapped in a debt for sins committed which they themselves could never redeem. Men and women of all stations and inclinations had trodden those paths since almost the very earliest Christian times – the earliest pilgrim narrative we have, the *Itinerarium Burdigalense*, recounts a pilgrimage from Bordeaux to Jerusalem in 333 or 334, and there is a vast number of narratives of pilgrimages to holy places – the most holy being Jerusalem and Rome, of course – that survive from the Middle Ages. So many of them have common features – like *quantifying* how much good a particular shrine might do you if approached in the right spirit of penitence and humility – that it's not too far off the mark to say that they make a recognizably distinct genre with its own conventions.

Be that as it may: pretty well everyone went on pilgrimage, from prince to peasant, pedlar to pauper, and it was the only place in mediaeval society (save the charnel house, as Will Langland points out) where a knight and a churl might rub shoulders on terms of semi-intimacy: Chaucer's fictional *Canterbury Tales* gives a wonderful picture of what being on a pilgrimage to Canterbury might be like.

Someone once said to me that in fifteenth century England it would have been hard to have gone to any village of any size and not to have found someone who had been at least as far as Rome: the English were notorious for gadding about. Pilgrimage was a journey you always took in company, for travel could be dangerous, and you would do it when the roads were less foul, in spring and summer: the holy-day season. People would gather in one of the bigger inns at the start of the journey – like Chaucer's Tabard in Southwark, pulled

down to make a fire break during a great fire in 1676. When
the group was big enough, they would set off led by someone
who knew the way – rather like the Master of the Caravan
in travel in the East.[47] Nor, as Chaucer's poem makes clear,
would the journey be all high thinking and spare feeding.
Then, as now, people's behaviour and motives would have been
mixed. William Thorpe, priest, examined for heresy before
Thomas Arundel, Archbishop of Canterbury, in 1407, roundly
condemned pilgrimages, for many the mediaeval equivalent of
the modern package tour – or, indeed, the cruise[48]:

*'Also, Sir, I know well, that when divers men and women
will go thus after their own wills, and finding out one
pilgrimage, they will ordain with them before[hand] to
have with them both men and women that can well sing
wanton songs; and some other pilgrims will have with
them bagpipes; so that every town that they come through,
what with the noise of their singing, and with the sound
of their piping, and with the jangling of their Canterbury
bells, and with the barking out of dogs after them, they
make more noise than if the King came there away, with
all his clarions and many other minstrels. And if these
men and women be a month out in their pilgrimage,*

---

[47] Maps in our sense did not exist, nor did signposts. The surname Palmer recalls
those folk who made a job out of going on pilgrimage as proxy for someone else:
they would know the way.

[48] In German the word is *kreuzfahrt*, 'cross journey', also 'crusade'. When I have
lectured on cruise ships, as I have done several times, I like to point this out.
People move away nervously.

many of them shall be, a half year after, great janglers, tale-tellers, and liars...'

And like Chaucer's Alison, the Wife of Bath, many of the single women, widows with legal disposal of what they had inherited from their husbands, would, as Chaucer, a shrewd poet, puts it, 'cross many a strange stream and know much of wandering by the way.' (She had been several times to Jerusalem and to Santiago da Compostela, and to Cologne.) Chaucer knew that people are never simple. The rascals and those out for a good time (no questions asked when you got home) would make up part of any little group of travellers. But that did not mean that Alison of Bath, say, or Robin the Miller would be any the less devout when they got to the actual shrine, did not say the requisite number of Aves and Pater Nosters. Just so (in my measure) when once I began to climb laboriously up a grassy field after fording a stream to where once the buildings of an ancient Priory stood, my mind was far less on kneeling before the Sacrament in the church than on having a long sit-down and a pint or two and a pie in the pub. But the two are not mutually exclusive, I thought: still think.

Bands of several dozen travellers arriving and needing food and shelter would strain the resources of any normal inn, and along the major routes the church built hospices, sometimes part of a monastery, sometimes remote where the travelling was hard and dangerous: like the Hospice at the top of the Great St Bernard Pass. It is easy to forget that it was not only people who needed feeding: their mounts needed fodder and stabling too. The Venetians (as always with their eye to profit), ran something like a regular summer ferry service from Venice to Jaffa. When you arrived at the holy place, again the church would have built hostels: much later, in the eleventh century, in the Holy Land, these were run by the Knights of St John, the Hospitallers, and later still by the Franciscans. What we moderns find extraordinary is that if you were poor you could do the whole stupendous journey relying entirely on the charity of the church for food and shelter. The monasteries, from very early times, had a duty to welcome wayfarers, and still do so: I have myself availed myself of it, and been welcomed by the brothers, and if you walk to the Hospital of St Cross in Winchester today, as mediaeval pilgrims on their way to venerate St Swithun's relics in the Cathedral would have done, you can still ask for the Wayfarer's Dole of bread and ale which was enjoined upon the foundation by the will of its founder, Henry of Blois, in the 12th century. Ely in the Middle Ages must have buzzed with voices speaking different varieties of English, and other tongues, for the shrine's appeal was wide, and the chance of a miraculous cure always to be hoped for. For, as Chaucer reminds us, in Spring,

Thanne longen folk to goon on pilgrimages,
And palmeres for to seken straunge strondes,
To ferne halwes, kowthe in sondry londes;
And specially from every shires ende
Of Engelond to Caunterbury they wende,
The hooly blisful martir for to seke,
That hem hath olpen whan that they were seeke.

He was thinking of St Thomas of Canterbury, of course. But Etheldreda had five centuries of head start as a specialist in diseases of the throat.

In the time of Nicholas West, Bishop from 1515 to 1533 (who built in the south-east corner of the cathedral the loveliest chantry chapel I know), in summer, and especially in June, Ely would have been bursting with people. They would be coming, like so many of their forebears, to do reverence to the relics, to file past the magnificent shrine of the royal saint, to take another step on their journey to Heaven. But clouds were building in their summer sky. When they broke, there came a deluge like none ever seen before.

CHAPTER 5

THE SPOILING OF ETHELDREDA

'... Ye shall purely and sincerely declare the very [true] Gospel of Christ, and in the same exhort your hearers to the works of charity, mercy, and faith, specially prescribed and commanded in Scripture, and not to repose their trust and affiance in any other works devised by men's phantasies besides Scripture; as in wandering to pilgrimages, offering of money, candles, or tapers to images or relics, or kissing or licking the same, saying over a number of beads, not understood or minded on...

... 7.Item, That such feigned images as ye know of in any of your cures to be so abused with pilgrimages or offerings of anything made thereunto, ye shall, for avoiding that most

detestable sin of idolatry, forthwith takedown and delay, and shall suffer from henceforth no candles, tapers, or images of wax to be set afore any image or picture but only the light that commonly goeth across the church by the rood-loft, the light before the sacrament of the altar, and the light about the sepulchre... which images, if they abuse for any other intent than for such remembrances, they commit idolatry in the same, to the great danger of their souls: and therefore the King's Highness, graciously tendering the weal of his subjects' souls, hath in part already, and more will hereafter, travail for the abolishing of such images as might be an occasion of so great an offence to God, and so great a danger to the souls of his loving subjects.'

Reform – and of course it was necessary, as everyone recognised, though perhaps not everybody agreed on what it was – had been in the air for some decades. New research into newly available Greek manuscripts of the Bible raised issues about interpretation, and about the authority of practices that had grown up over centuries. And after all, the Gospels are inherently subversive of *all* power structures and complacent customs and thinking.

There were the palpable abuses that any old institution develops when the original ethos behind a practice has been forgotten; there was the clash between the authority of the priest and the Church and the intelligence and integrity of the individual. There was too easy an equation in many people's minds that salvation was less of an act of Divine grace than of a monetary transaction brokered by the church...

For most people, these were heady issues best left to the scholars, and this summary is a gross oversimplification of many complex issues. There are volumes more to say. But it is enough for now to say the world was turned upside down for the vast majority of people who were suddenly told that what they had always known, had believed, and been used to doing, often with love, what had been part of the cement holding a society together, was wrong and they had to stop it immediately. No more seeking the intercession of a beloved saint as of a friend... For so many, the top-down Reformation was a terrible and painful time. For some others, it was extremely profitable.

Thomas Cromwell, the deplorable Henry VIII's chief minister after the disgrace of Cardinal Wolsey, wrote the Royal Injunctions from which those words on the opposite page are taken. They went out to every parish in 1538. They are concomitant with the dissolution of the monasteries by a set of administrative and legal processes between 1536 and 1541 that disbanded monasteries, priories, convents, and friaries in all his dominions, expropriated to the Crown's use – and debts – their income, sold off their assets. (It is at least a small recompense that former monks and priests were given pensions – which were paid, in some cases for decades.) Those who resisted (and many did, openly or in secret, in fear of the informer), were treated harshly, sometimes with extreme cruelty.

Religion allied with secular power is a toxic mix. Henry's realm drank it by the gallon: he made himself first Supreme Governor then Head of the Church, and the English Bible issued in his reign, which every parish church had to buy, had him dominant on the title page. The shrines were wrecked, pulled down, the bones and relics of saints scattered to the four winds or thrown on the midden – anything of value, of course, being sold, even to the very stones of the walls and the nails from the timbers of the roof: to clear the debt of the Crown, to enrich the parvenu or the favourite, to buy a jewel for a wanton ambling nymph.

A high profile shrine like Etheldreda's at Ely suffered too, of course, just like anywhere else. The destruction was rapid and complete, perhaps because Prior Robert Wells and the 23 monks who signed the Deed of Surrender on 18 November 1539 supported the iconoclastic ideas of the Reformation. Many of them did take positions in the new church – some refused – but of course that is not necessarily indication of moral or theological conviction: it may simply have been a bending with the political wind. The actual spoiling probably came soon after Bishop Goodrich's instruction to the clergy of his diocese on 21 October 1541, commanding the immediate destruction of 'all images, relicks, table monuments of miracles and shrines.' Some 361 ounces of pure gold, and 5040 ounces of gold and silver plate, were sent into the bottomless pit of the royal treasury.

Tiny bits of the fabric of the shrine may survive: some think a small bit of a possibly eighth-century carved frieze in a barn wall at St. John's Farm might come from the shrine. It is not known what sort of state her body was in when it was finally removed from that sarcophagus the monks brought from the ruins of Roman Durolipons – or what happened to the sarcophagus itself. Her relics, like Thomas Becket's or St Edmund's, were scattered to the four winds or burned. A 900 year tradition of worship and honour vanished in a week.

Sometimes, individuals, risking much, tried to save part at least of what they loved: a beautiful retable of (probably) Thetford Priory, was hidden in a cowshed, and found again sixty years ago, and now graces Thornham Parva church in Suffolk. Three panels from a spectacular Netherlandish altarpiece which has been owned by Queens' College, Cambridge, at least since 1717 (ultimate provenance unknown), match exactly the description of one in Long Melford Church, Suffolk, in *The Spoil of Melford Church.* That sad chronicle of destruction was written by Roger Martin, Churchwarden at the time the Instructions were sent and the commissioners from London arrived to do their work.

A retable of about 1455 showing Etheldreda's marriages and the finding of her incorrupt body, which was almost certainly in her shrine chapel, is now in the care of the Society of Antiquaries of London. A Fellow of that Society, Thomas Kerrich, was given them in 1792 by the antiquary Rev. James Bentham (1708–94), who had found them by chance many years earlier in a house in Ely, reused as cupboard doors. And sometimes, bits of the actual saints were squirrelled away, revered in secret. In Brixworth, Northamptonshire, someone cared enough to hide a reliquary in a wall. Perhaps he was hoping that when his world recovered its senses he would recover it, and he must have had one or two helpers.

He never did recover it. It was forgotten, until a few years ago a builder engaged on some repair found it. In it is a hyoid bone – it looks just like the sort of chicken bone I dig up in my garden – and we know that Offa, who ruled Mercia from 757 to 796, gave to that church the throat bone of St Boniface, Apostle of the Germans, martyred in Frisia in 754. This little brown bone I was being shown once vibrated to a saint's voice when he commanded the felling of Donner's (Thor's) Oak in Hesse. It was a strange, curiously matter of fact moment, that first time I saw a real relic... and unforgettable as you see.

Another example: found in a priest hole in a house in Arundel, Sussex, in about 1811 was a reliquary, inside which was a shrivelled left hand on a silver plate, on which was engraved *Manus Sanctae Etheldredae DCLXXIII*, ('The Hand of St Etheldreda 1573'). The plate was of a tenth century style, which might suggest the hand was separated from its body about then.

In a lecture given at St Etheldreda's in Ely Place, Holborn, in March 1876, the antiquarian Alexander Wood said that when the hand was found it was 'perfectly entire and quite white [but] exposure to the air has now changed it to a dark brown and the skin has cracked and disappeared in several places'. It was given to the Duke of Norfolk – the Howards of Norfolk stayed Catholic through many vicissitudes – and then passed down to the community of Dominican Sisters at Stone, and finally, since 1953, has been held in St Etheldreda's RC church in Egremont Street in Ely. A small part of it has been venerated in St Etheldreda's, Holborn. There, for a long time, was the London residence of the Bishops of Ely, and it was within the jurisdiction not of the City but of that palatinate jurisdiction which descends from Tondberct to the saint herself.

But: in soil, that infinitely complex powerhouse on which we all depend, you can't ever quite get rid of mycelium: *naturam expellas furca, tamen usque recurret*, 'you can chuck nature out with a pitchfork, but it will soon hurry back', says Horace. Even so with that need for spiritual sustenance at the centre of what it is to be human and conscious, a need for which we have no name. So Walsingham, Canterbury, Lindisfarne, Glastonbury, Ely and many other places never quite lost their hold on the imagination and memory even when what you were remembering them for was indistinct, nebulous, even dismissed as superstitious (the root mean of which word in Latin is, ironically, 'survival.') The old shrines, the old relics, are no longer there but their places still draw people. Little by little, footfall by tentative footfall, the pilgrims have come back – not in curiosity, or as mere antiquarians – perish the thought! – but as searchers for that which they acknowledge but cannot comprehend or even verbalise. Pilgrims once more flock to Walsingham, even though the new shrine built a hundred years ago is a good way from the ruins of the old one. They make their way to the shrine of the Black Virgin of Willesden, the parish given to the monks of Westminster by Æthelstan in 938.[49]

Even as I write this, I think of a new/ancient pilgrimage the Reformers thought they had got rid of: St Eanswyð, granddaughter of Æthelbert of Kent, sister of St Æethelburh, Edwin of Northumbria's holy queen, died (around 650) no older than 22, having refused marriage and founded the first

---

[49] Thomas Cromwell's men dragged the original image to which St Thomas More made his pilgrimage, shortly before he was beheaded by the king he had loved and served well, to Chelsea, where More's home was, and burnt it in 1538.

women's convent in England at Folkestone. Her relics, objects of devotion for nine hundred years, were hidden away in a reliquary made of re-used Roman lead in the walls of the twelfth century Priory church to which they had been translated, and all that was mortal of her slept there until builders found the urn in 1885. Recent osteoarchaeological, C^{14} and DNA analysis has made as sure as ever may be that these are her remains, and already pilgrims, especially from the Orthodox churches of Eastern Europe, are making their way there. Pilgrims make their way to Ely again, and to Ely Place. Only the other week, someone in the Cathedral said to me, *à propos* of that hand, 'We really would quite like it back.'

But you can never recover what the past was, you can't un-be what has been and what has made you: you have to use the past to make a new thing. We go on from here, we are on a new journey. For we are all pilgrims, and God knows the world needs healing.

Thanks

This book grew out of an idea that came out of nowhere one January day as the dog – a yellow Labrador by the name of Milo, if you are interested – was paddling in the water of the unkempt, dank little pond on the Golf Course at Ely that some think is/was Etheldreda's Well. He was stirring up all sorts of things while I waited for him to finish. So the first person to thank is Milo. And he has been a patient companion sitting by or under the desk while I have been furiously writing. The book had to be written quickly, for the 1350th anniversary of the founding of Etheldreda's Abbey loomed very close.

The second lot of really heartfelt thanks is due to my publishers, who picked up this ball and ran with it with a cheerful efficiency I wish was emulated by all. The best recognition and appreciation that can be given them is for you to buy the book and read it. Then, thanks to all those many people who guaranteed to buy a copy even before there was a word on my screen and only a wild gleam in my eye. Among them was Dr Virginia Warren, who read the eventual MS at speed with meticulous care, made so many helpful suggestions, and saved me from one or two gross errors, including one about exhumations.

I also owe so much to my dear friend and colleague, Professor Helen Cooper, who read and commented with her usual acuteness on the whole MS in the interstices of tiresome work on proofs of a second edition of her work on Chaucer. And she did it with an alacrity and speed for which I shall ever be grateful.

But the biggest thanks must go to Rosanna my wife, once more a writing widow – 'would you get me a coffee, beloved?' – and my most perceptive critic.

CWRDM   Ely, Sexagesima, MMXXIII

Some of the People in the Story
− or this part of it, for stories have no end

*= has an entry of their own

Æthelbert, king of Kent, r. c. 589-616, m. Bercta or Bertha, daughter of Charibert I of Francia. Father of Æthelburh* and Eanswyð.

Æthelburh of the East Angles, daughter of Anna*, sister of our heroine, nun, and later Abbess at Faremoutiers-en-Brie.

Æthelburh of Kent, daughter of Æthelbert and Bercta, b. ca.601, m. Edwin* of Northumbria 625, mother of Eanflaed*.

Æthelfrith, king of Bernicia, defeated and killed by Rædwald* at the Battle of the River Idle in 616.

Æbbe, c. 615-83, daughter of Æthelfrith* and Acha*, sister of Oswald* and Oswiu*, founded monasteries at Ebchester and Coldingham.

Ælle, d.588, first king of Deira after it broke from Bernicia's overlordship in 560. Father of Edwin*, Acha* and one other son (Pope Gregory made a hopeful pun on 'Aelle' and 'Alleluia').

Æthelhere, Anna's* brother, Etheldreda's uncle, took over as king when Anna was killed by Penda* near Blythburgh in 653/4 and was himself killed fighting for Penda in 655 at the battle of the Winwæd.

Æthelwold, 904/9-984, Abbot of Abingdon, made by Dunstan* Bp of Winchester 963-84, one of the leaders of the tenth-century monastic reforms, refounded Ely as a Benedictine all-male monastery.

Acha, daughter of Ælle* of Deira, sister of Edwin*, m. Æthelfrith* king of Bernicia. Mother of Eanfrith of Bernicia (590–634), Oswald* of Northumbria (c. 604-642) Oswiu* of Northumbria (c. 612-670).

Aidan, d.651. Founded (with Edwin's* gift) the monastery of Lindisfarne (635). Trained at Iona.

Alcuin of York, c.735-804, taught by Bede,* trained at York, founded the Palace School at Charlemagne's invitation at his capital, Aachen.

Anna (or Ona), king of the East Angles from c. 640 until killed by Penda* 653/4. Devout father of several saints. He acceded to the throne after his father Eni, brother of Rædwald*, was killed by Penda.

Augustine of Canterbury, Prior of a monastery in Rome, chosen by Pope Gregory* the Great in 595 to lead a mission to Kent. Died in 604.

Bede, 672?-735. Joined the monastery at Monkwearmouth aged 7, became one of the most learned and influential scholars of his and any time. His *Historia Ecclesiastica Gentis Anglorum* is one the chief literary sources for our knowledge of the period.

Bercta, Merovingian princess, d. of Charibert 1 of Francia, m. Æthelbert* of Kent.

Columba, 521-97, prince of the Northern O'Neills of Ulster, founded the very influential monastery of Iona 563.

Cuthbert, c. 634-687, of noble birth and perhaps bred to the profession of arms, decided after a vision on the night of Aidan's death in 651 to become a monk. Trained at Melrose, a daughter monastery of Iona, of which he became Prior, then later became Bishop of Lindisfarne.

Cynefrith, physician to Etheldreda.

Dunstan, 909-88, became Archbishop of Canterbury in 960. Minister and mentor of several English Kings, including the great Æthelstan, the first king who could realistically call himself King of all England. As archbishop the force behind major ecclesiastical reforms.

Eanflæd, 626-685, daughter of Edwin*, granddaughter of Æthelbert* of Kent, married Oswiu*.

Ecgfrith, c. 645-685, our heroine's second chaste husband, son of Oswiu* and Eanflæd*.

Edwin of Northumbria, r.616-633, elder son of Ælle*, defeated and killed by Penda* at Hatfield Chase in 633. (And see p105.)

Ermenhild, daughter of Seaxburh*, m. Wulhere of Mercia (Christian son of pagan Penda*), 3rd Abbess of Ely.

Etheldreda, our heroine.

Gregory the Great, 540-604, Pope 590-604. One of the four great Fathers of the Western church (the others are Jerome, Augustine (of Hippo), Ambrose.

Guthlac, 674-714, Mercian nobleman, retired as a hermit to Crowland.

Hild, 614-80, second daughter of Hereric, nephew of Edwin*, and brought up at Edwin's court when her father was poisoned. Founded Abbey at Whitby.

Oswald, King of Northumbria, r.633-642, killed by Penda* at Maserfield. Nephew of Edwin*, grandson of Ælle*.

Oswiu, (r. 642-67) brother of and successor to Oswald*. Defeated Penda* at the battle of the Winwæd. Called the Synod of Whitby (664).

Ovin, Steward to Etheldreda.

Paulinus (d.644) one of the second mission sent by Gregory in 604, travelled north to Edwin* with Æthelburh* of Kent, converted Edwin, also baptised Hild*. First Bishop of York.

Penda, d.655, King of Mercia, pagan, in 628 took over the whole of the Severn Valley after the battle of Cirencester and defeated and, in alliance with Cadwallon the Christian king of Gwynedd, killed Edwin* of Northumbria at Hatfield Chase in 633. Defeated and killed Oswald* of Northumbria at Maserfield in 642, and after this was perhaps the most powerful ruler in the Seven Kingdoms of the English. He drove the Christian king of Wessex, Cenwalh, into exile with Anna*, and often defeated the East Angles. He killed Etheldreda's father and brother near Blythburgh in 653. Finally he was killed by forces led by Oswiu* at the Battle of the Winwæd, 655. A military genius.

Rædwald (r.599-624) Initially he ruled under the overlordship of Æthelbert* of Kent, at whose court he converted to Christianity (604). In 616, after defeating and killing Æthelfrith* of Northumbria in the Battle of the River Idle, he had the power to install Edwin*, who had been a fugitive in exile at his court, as king of Northumbria. During the battle, both Æthelfrith* and Rædwald's own son, Rægenhere, were killed. He was just about the most powerful king in the Seven Kingdoms after this. Unusually for kings at this time, he seems to have died in his bed, and it may be him for whom the great ship burial at Sutton Hoo was made.

Seaxburh, (d.699) a formidable woman of great organising and PR ability. Queen of Kent, then abbess of her foundation at Minster-in-Sheppey. Succeeded her younger sister Etheldreda as Abbess of Ely.

Tondberct, d.655, earldorman or prince of the Southern Gyrwas, first husband of Etheldreda and ally of Anna*.

Wihtburh, Abbess of Dereham, reputedly another sister of Etheldreda, but the usual date given for her death (743) makes this unlikely.

Wilfrid 633-709/10, Bishop. A Northumbrian noble, entered religious life in his teens, studied at Lindisfarne, Canterbury and Rome. Returned to Northumbria c. 660, became abbot of Ripon. At Synod of Whitby (664) argued powerfully for the Roman position. Oswiu's* second son, Alhfrith, made him Bishop of Northumbria. He was consecrated in Francia. Alhfrith led an unsuccessful revolt against his father, leaving a question mark over Wilfrid's appointment, and before Wilfrid's return Oswiu* had appointed Ceadda (Chad) in his stead. Wilfrid retired to Ripon. After becoming Archbishop of Canterbury in 668 Theodore of Tarsus deposed Ceadda (who went to Lichfield) and restored Wilfrid as Bishop of Northumbria. Quarrelled with Ecgfrith* over Etheldreda, was expelled from York, went to Selsey in West Sussex. Patched up a relationship with Ecgfrith's successor, Aldfrith, but they quarrelled in 692 and Wilfrid went to Mercia. Finally, reconciled, he got back his monasteries of Ripon and Hexham.

Timelines

597: the first mission, under Augustine, sent by Gregory the Great, to Æthelberht of Kent.

604: the second, led by Paulinus (later the first Bishop of York).

c. 610-635: The Burial in Mound 1 at Sutton Hoo: Rædwald of East Anglia (r. 599-624)?

617: Battle of the River Idle: According to Bede, Edwin, son of Aelle, king of Deira, was driven out of the kingdom by Æthelfric of Bernicia, and took refuge with Rædwald. Rædwald resisted demands by Æthelfric's successor, that he kill Edwin. Instead he joined forces with Edwin at the river Idle, where they won a great victory. Edwin was put on the throne of Northumbria.

630-670: The burial at Harpole, Northamptonshire.

c 670-700: The 'Burial of the Princess' at Ely.

633: Battle of Hatfield Chase: Edwin of Northumbria killed by Penda.

636-654: reign of Anna of East Anglia: killed by Penda near Blythburgh.

636: Birth of Etheldreda.

633-648: St Felix active in East Anglia.

652: Etheldreda's marriage to Tondberct.

645?: Birth of Ecgfrith son of Oswiu.

655: Tondberct's death.

655: Battle of the Winwæd: Oswiu (r. 642-67) victorious; death of Penda of Mercia.

660: Etheldreda's marriage to Ecgfrith; meets Wilfrid of York.

672: Etheldreda's withdrawal to Aebbe's monastery.

673: Etheldreda returns to Ely, founds the monastery.

679: Etheldreda's death; her elder sister Seaxburh, formerly queen of Kent, becomes Abbess.

695: Translation of Etheldreda's remains: the cult begins to grow.

c. 731: Bede's *History* completed.

793: First Viking attack on Lindisfarne.

870: The Great Heathen Army winters at Torksey, and part of it ravages the Fens, burning Soham Abbey and the monastery at Ely.

878: Ælfred forces them to the peace of Wedmore, and Guthorm the Danish leader accepts baptism. The treaty effectively partitioned the kingdom. (The Danelaw covers much of northern and eastern England.)

960: Dunstan (*ob.* 988) becomes Archbishop of Canterbury, commences reform of the England church.

970: Æthelwold (his friend and colleague, Bishop of Winchester), refounds the Ely monastery as an all-male Benedictine house, and commences building a new stone church.

1066: the defeat of the English at Hastings. Resistance in the Fens, based in Ely.

1071: The monks make peace with William I.

1081: Abbot Simeon starts the rebuilding of the monastery on a very grand scale indeed. Building of the new nave starts.

1109: Ely made a bishopric; the monastery now has a Prior not an Abbot. The Abbot, Hervé le Breton, becomes the first Bishop.

Late 1100s: The commissioning of the *Liber Eliensis*.

1534: Henry VIII's break with Rome; makes himself Head of the Church; ascendancy of Thomas Cromwell.

1536-40: Suppression and dissolution of the monasteries.

1538: The Royal Injunctions issued.

1539: Henry dissolves the Monastery and Cathedral. Most communal buildings destroyed.

1541: Destruction of Etheldreda's shrine; the church not destroyed as it was the seat of a bishop. Had it not been, it would have been pulled down, and left a ruin like Fountains or Rievaulx for English Heritage to look after.

1541: Henry establishes a new Foundation, and the Cathedral becomes The Cathedral Church of the Holy and Undivided Trinity at Ely.

1610: last Saint's Life of Etheldreda, by Ralph (or Robert) Buckland in British Library MS Stowe 949, *Lives of Women Saints of our Contrie of England*, never printed until the mid 1880s.

1792: panels (of c. 1455), showing scenes of Etheldreda's life, found being used as cupboard doors in a house in Ely, given to Society of Antiquaries of London.

1811: Discovery at Arundel of her hand, (hidden 1573?) given by the Duke of Norfolk to the Dominican Sisters at Stone.

1835: and later: Abolition of the Palatinate jurisdictions.

1953: The hand is given to St Etheldreda's RC church in Ely.

THE SEVEN KINGDOMS OF THE ENGLISH

In the seventh century, the land that came to be called England was divided between the Seven Kingdoms of the English. Parts of the west and north of modern England and southern Scotland were still held by the Welsh and the Cornish. The Seven Kingdoms were Kent, Wessex, Mercia, Essex, East Anglia, Sussex, and the land north of the Humber, Northumbria. The king who was for a time the most powerful among them was called Bretwalda, 'wide ruler', or 'ruler of Britain'.

But the land north of the Humber, the land of the Angles, was initially divided between the smaller realms of Bernicia and Deira, each with its own royal dynasty. Ælle ruled Deira until his death in 588. His children were a daughter, Acha, his son Edwin, and another son whose name is forgotten. The Bernician dynasty, allied in kinship to the house of Wessex, came to dominate Deira. In various squabbles (a trivial word, but not trivial to them) Æthelfrith king of Bernicia invaded Deira in 604, and deposed Edwin the heir, his own wife Acha's brother, who fled to exile in the court of Cadfan ap Iago of Gwynedd. By the 610s Edwin was in Mercia with king Cearl, whose daughter Cwenburg he married (she died in 625). By 616, he was in East Anglia under Rædwald's protection. Bede says that Æthelfrith tried to have Rædwald murder his rival, and that Rædwald's wife persuaded him to hold his hand. It came to the arbitrament. of arms: by the river Idle, Æthelfrith was killed by Rædwald in 616. Rædwald installed Edwin as king of all Northumbria. Æthelfrith›s children, potential rivals, to Edwin

– and his nephews and niece – fled: Æbbe with her mother and brother Oswald and Oswiu to the court of Eochaid mac Buidhe in Dal Riata. At the heart of Dal Riata was Iona, and it was during their exile that she and her brothers converted to Christianity. Under her younger brother, Oswiu, the northern and southern kingdoms were finally united in Northumbria.

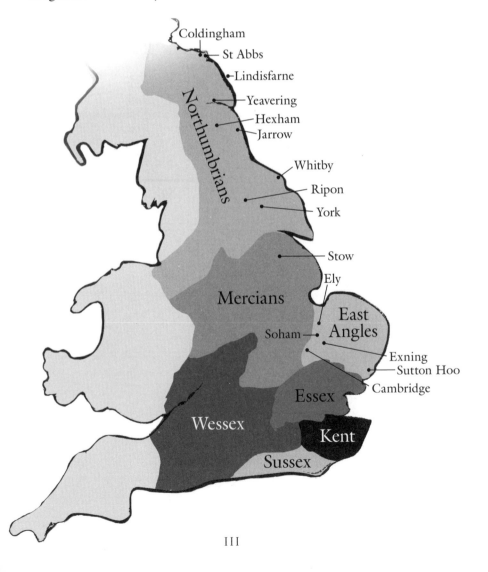

✝ THE FAMILY BUSINESS

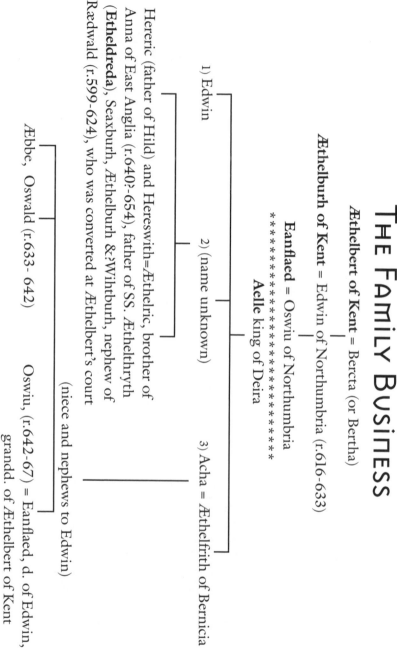

Æthelbert of Kent = Bercta (or Bertha)

Æthelburh of Kent = Edwin of Northumbria (r.616-633)

****

Eanflæd = Oswiu of Northumbria

****

Aelle king of Deira

1) Edwin

2) (name unknown)

3) Acha = Æthelfrith of Bernicia

Hereric (father of Hild) and Hereswith=Æthelric, brother of Anna of East Anglia (r.640?-654), father of SS. Æthelthryth (**Etheldreda**), Seaxburh, Æthelburh &:Wihtburh, nephew of Rædwald (r.599-624), who was converted at Æthelbert's court

Æbbe, Oswald (r.633- 642)

(niece and nephews to Edwin)

Oswiu, (r.642-67) = Eanflæd, d. of Edwin, grandd. of Æthelbert of Kent

Ecgfrith of Nothumbria